MEDIA

River

BABYLON

UR

PERSIAN GULF

ARABIA

N

E

W

S

New CATHOLIC PICTURE BIBLE

POPULAR STORIES FROM THE OLD AND NEW TESTAMENTS

By

REV. LAWRENCE G. LOVASIK, S.V.D.

Divine Word Missionary

Illustrated

CATHOLIC BOOK PUBLISHING COMPANY
NEW YORK

Foreword

THE **Old Testament** tells of several promises which God made to man before the coming of our Lord, especially of the promise which was made to the Children of Israel at Mount Sinai.

All through this story there runs the great promise of the Messias. Even though Israel was unfaithful, God was true to His word. We read how He restored some of the nation to Palestine and how He encouraged the Jews to prepare for the coming of the Redeemer.

In the Gospel Story of the **New Testament** Jesus shows Himself to you as He lived on earth—in His teaching and in His love. You can be pleasing to God only insofar as your life is lived after His teaching and example.

This PICTURE BIBLE will help you to know the goodness of God and His great love for people. It will help you to know Jesus better, that you may love Him, and follow His example more closely. The pictures in full color will make His life more real in your mind. Read the life of Jesus often, and pray to Him as you read it, for it is especially through prayer that you can obtain the grace to become like Jesus.

To Jesus Christ, the Divine Word, Who called Himself "the Way, the Truth, and the Life," through the most pure hands of His loving Mother and ours, these pages are gratefully and affectionately dedicated.

Fr. Lawrence S.V.D.

NIHIL OBSTAT: Daniel V. Flynn, J.C.D. — *Censor Librorum*

IMPRIMATUR: Joseph T. O'Keefe — *Vicar General, Archdiocese of New York*

(T-435)

4 5 6 7 8 9 10 11 12 13 14 15

✝ CONTENTS ✝

Contents — Continued —

The Old Testament

THE story which we read in the Old Testament really begins when Moses led the Israelites out of Egypt and formed them into a nation. Moses wished to explain to the Israelites just how this had come about. So he wrote for them the early story of the human race, how God made the world and man, how sin and suffering had come, and how mankind was destroyed in the flood. Then he showed how the Children of Israel came to be chosen as the special nation of God. Moses gave this new nation its laws and its religious customs. He then led them on toward the Promised Land.

The rest of the story tells how the Children of Israel served or did not serve God, from the time they went into the Promised Land until just before the coming of Jesus. At Mount Sinai God had made a promise to this people that He would protect them and have them as His special nation. He gave many favors and blessings to the Children of Israel; He kept before them the hope of the **Messiah.** But the Children of Israel became weak. They often fell into evil. In punishment, their kingdom was finally destroyed.

God is the Creator of heaven and earth, and of all things.

1. THE STORY OF THE CREATION

GOD is eternal. He had no beginning, and He will have no end. God made the angels. They are spirits like the soul of man.

Lucifer was one of the most glorious and most beautiful of the angels. His name means "Bearer of Light." He became very proud and even wanted to be as great as God Himself. He cried out against God, "I will not serve!" With him were other angels who also refused to obey God.

But the Archangel Michael cried out, "Who is like God?" Other good angels joined him in a great battle against Lucifer and his bad angels, and drove the bad ones into a place of eternal punishment. We call Lucifer "Satan," and his bad angels "devils."

To have a fitting place for man to live, God made the universe.

On the **first** day God made earth out of nothing. Then God said, "Let light be made," and at once light appeared. God separated light from darkness and called them day and night.

On the **second** day God made the blue sky and called it heaven.

On the **third** day God said, "Let the waters under heaven be gathered together into one place, and let the dry land appear. Let this dry land bring forth grass and trees and plants of every kind."

On the **fourth** day God made the sun, the moon, and the stars.

On the **fifth** day God made the fishes and other creatures that were to live in the water. He also made birds and other creatures that were to fly in the sky.

On the **sixth** day God made all the animals that were to live on the ground. Then God said, "I shall make man in My image. I shall make man to rule over all the things that I have created." God formed man out of the dust of the earth. Then He breathed into him a soul that will never die.

On the **seventh** day God rested from His work. He blessed that day and made it holy.

Adam and Eve are driven out of Paradise because of their sin.

2. ADAM AND EVE IN PARADISE

GOD called the first man Adam. Adam had an extremely clear and bright mind. He loved God and tried in every way to please Him. God told Adam to rule all other creatures.

Since God wanted Adam to be happy, He planted a beautiful Garden, called the Garden of Eden or Paradise, for him to live in. There were all kinds of trees, plants, flowers, and fruits in this Garden. Beasts and birds came to Adam, and he gave them names.

In the middle of the Garden, God also planted the Tree of Knowledge of good and evil. God said to Adam, "You may eat of the fruit of every other tree in the Garden, but you must not eat the fruit of the Tree of Knowledge of good and evil. If you eat of it, you shall die."

God put Adam to sleep, and taking one of his ribs, formed out of it a woman. When Adam awoke, God gave him the woman for his companion. Her name was Eve, which means "Mother of all the living."

Adam and Eve were very happy in Paradise because they loved God and were in God's grace. The Tree of Life kept them from sickness and death. They were to live forever.

Adam had all that he wanted. He knew that he would always be happy as long as he served God. He was to pass his happiness on to all who came after him. But he had to be tested to prove that he was worthy of this great blessing.

Satan was jealous. He tempted Eve to disobey God one day when she was near the Tree of Knowledge of good and evil. He came to her in the form of a serpent and said to her, "You shall not die if you eat the fruit of this Tree. You will be like God, knowing good and evil."

Eve was led into sin because she listened to the devil. She ate the fruit and gave some to Adam, who also ate. At once they were filled with shame and fear.

God called Adam and Eve, and asked them why they had eaten of the forbidden fruit. They tried to excuse themselves.

After God told Adam that he would have to work hard all the days of his life, and that he and his wife would have to die, He expelled them from the Garden of Paradise.

Then God said to the serpent, "I will put hatred between you and the woman . . . She shall crush your head." God promised that the rule of Satan over mankind would be broken by the Child whom a woman would bring into the world. This Child was to be the Redeemer of the human race, and the Blessed Virgin Mary would be His Mother.

Cain becomes jealous when he sees that Abel's gifts are more pleasing to God than his own.

3. CAIN AND ABEL

ADAM and Eve soon saw how much evil their sin would bring upon the earth. Adam had to work hard to keep himself and Eve alive. He had to hunt for food.

The first children of Adam and Eve were Cain and Abel. Cain grew up to be a farmer and Abel became a shepherd. Cain was cruel and Abel was kind.

Cain and Abel offered gifts to God as a sacrifice. Cain offered fruit and grain; Abel offered a lamb of his flock.

When God saw that Cain's heart was full of evil, He was not pleased with his gifts. But God was pleased with Abel's gifts because his heart was full of goodness, and he offered his gifts to God with a better spirit. This made Cain very jealous. He determined to kill his brother. One day when they were walking in the field, Cain struck his brother and killed him.

The first murder had been committed. Then Adam learned what death meant.

God asked Cain, "Where is your brother Abel?"

He answered, "I do not know. Am I my brother's keeper?"

God was angry and said, "The voice of your brother's blood cries out to Me. You shall be cursed, and you shall be a wanderer upon the earth."

Hearing how he was to be punished, Cain cried out, "My sin is too great to be forgiven. I must hide myself from Your face. Anyone who finds me will kill me." But God put a mark upon Cain as a sign that no one should kill him. Cain began to wander over the earth and to suffer for his sin.

God gave Adam another son, called Seth, who grew up to be a good man. His children honored God and lived according to His laws, and they were called the children of God. Through Seth the worship of the true God, with the hope of the Redeemer, came down to other people who were to live many years later.

But the children of Cain grew up to be bad. Many centuries passed. The human race grew both in numbers and in knowledge of the things which make life easier. Some of the children of Cain built a city; others lived in tents. In this way the first cities began, and men learned to live with one another. They learned to plant and grow things and to make the animals carry their burdens. But they forgot God.

After a while the children of Cain began to marry the children of Seth. The sons and daughters born to these parents also became bad. Men began to have many wives. They worshipped the sun and the earth as gods. They made statues, called them gods, and even worshipped them. Evil spread through the whole human race. Man became very wicked.

Noah offers a sacrifice to God in thanksgiving.

4. NOAH'S ARK

WHEN God saw how men forgot and disobeyed Him, He said, "I will destroy them and all other living creatures."

Among the wicked people there lived a good man, Noah, who still loved God. Noah had three sons — Shem, Ham, and Japheth. With their wives they also were true to God. God said to Noah, "Because men have turned away from Me, I will send rain for forty days. A great flood shall rise to wipe away every living creature from the earth. But because you honor

Me, I shall spare you. Build an ark of wood. When it is finished, take your wife, your sons, and their families, and enter the ark, that you may be saved."

Noah believed the word of God. He and his sons at once set about making the ark. They built an ark which was three stories high and divided into little rooms. It took Noah over one hundred years to finish the work. Then Noah went into the ark with his family and seven pairs of certain animals, and two pairs of the other animals. He also carried enough food into the ark, and closed the door of the ark.

For forty days and forty nights heavy rain fell and flooded the land. The waters rose higher and higher till even the mountains were covered. Every living thing—bird, beast, and man—was drowned.

After forty days the rain stopped, but the water remained on the earth for one hundred and fifty days. Then the flood went down, and the ark rested on the top of a mountain. Noah sent out a dove three times. When it did not return the third time, Noah knew that the waters no longer covered the earth. So Noah with his family, and all living creatures, stepped out upon the dry land. Noah was thankful, and he built an altar and offered a sacrifice to God.

Because Noah was obedient, God was pleased with him and his family. He promised that there would never be another flood. God placed a rainbow in the sky as a sign of His promise.

God made a new promise to Noah. He promised that He would bring mankind again into His favor, if men would worship Him alone and be faithful to His service. God also gave him the hope of the Redeemer. To his son Shem, and to those who came after him, fell the great task of protecting the worship of the true God and the promise of the Messiah.

Abram welcomes three strangers into his home, who are really God and two angels.

5. THE PROMISE TO ABRAM

(2,000 B.C.)

PEOPLE began to forget God on whom all things depend. They made false gods. They adored them and prayed to them. But God did not destroy them as He had done in the deluge. Instead, He chose from the family of Shem a man known for his faith. His name was Abram.

Abram, in spite of the evils about him, had kept himself faithful to the service of God. One day God said to him, "Abram, leave your country, and go to the Land of Canaan."

Abram obeyed God and began his long journey to Canaan with his wife Sarah, his nephew Lot, and his helpers and flocks.

God picked Canaan as a home for Abram because these valleys were the great centers where men lived.

God rewarded Abram by making this promise: "I will give you and your children the Land of Canaan. You shall be the father of a great people. Through you all nations shall be blessed." Because of this promise, the Land of Canaan was called "The Promised Land." We now call it Palestine.

God was very good to Abram at Canaan. He gave him great riches. His flocks grew very large. But Abram had no children. Abram prayed to God, "Shall I die without children? Shall I have to give all my riches to the son of one of my servants?"

God heard Abram's prayer. One hot day three strangers came to Abram's tent. He welcomed them and gave them food. One of the strangers told Abram that in a year he would return and by that time Sarah would have a son.

Inside the tent Sarah heard this and laughed to herself. "Shall I have a son," she said, "when I am old, and my husband also is old?"

One of the strangers said to Abram, "Why did Sarah laugh? Is anything too hard for the Lord?"

At these words Abram knew that God Himself had come to him with two angels.

Abram trusted God and waited for a son. One day God said to him, "From now on your name shall be Abraham, because you shall be the father of many nations . . . I will keep My promise and give you a son. I will bless him. He shall be the father of kings and nations. You shall name him Isaac."

In these words, God had in mind not only Isaac, who was born not long after, but also the Messiah. Isaac was to carry on the promise, and his son Jacob was to do the same, and his family after him, until the Redeemer was born. This was the Savior whom God had promised when He expelled Adam and Eve from the Garden of Paradise. He was to make men happy by bringing them back to God's friendship.

An angel stops Abraham from killing his son Isaac.

6. ABRAHAM'S SACRIFICE

WHEN Abraham was a hundred years old, Sarah gave him a son. They called him "Isaac," meaning "Laughter," for Sarah said, "God has made me laugh, and everyone who hears of it shall laugh with me."

Abraham and Sarah loved Isaac with all their hearts because he had been sent as God had promised, to make them happy in their old age. But God wanted to test Abraham, to see whether he loved his son more than he loved God. One night God said to Abraham, "Take Isaac and go to a mountain that I shall show you. There offer me your son as a sacrifice."

Abraham became very sad. As he had always obeyed God, he was ready to obey Him now. He cut wood for the sacrifice. With two servants and his son, he set out to find the place that God would show him.

After three days they came to a mountain called Mount Moriah. Abraham said to his servants, "Stay here while Isaac and I go up the mountain to offer a sacrifice."

Abraham placed the wood upon the shoulders of Isaac, while he himself carried the fire and a knife. As they were going up the mountain, Isaac asked, "Father, we have the fire and wood, but where is the victim for the sacrifice?"

His father answered, "God will give us a victim for the sacrifice."

When they came to the place for the sacrifice, they made an altar and put the wood upon it. Then Abraham tied Isaac and laid him upon the wood.

Just as Abraham was about to strike his son with the knife, an angel touched his hand and said, "Abraham, do not kill your son. God knows now that you truly love Him, for you are ready to sacrifice Isaac at His command."

These words made Abraham very happy. He saw a sheep caught in the bushes. He took the sheep and offered it to God as a sacrifice, instead of his son.

Then the angel told Abraham that God would bless him for this offering he had made, that he would have very many descendants, and that from his family the Savior of the world would one day be born.

Isaac carrying the wood up the mountain is a picture of Jesus who carried His cross up the hill to Calvary, to offer Himself for the sins of the world. Although God saved Abraham's son, for love of us He did not save His own Son from death.

God said to Abraham, "I will bless you. And in your family shall all the nations of the earth be blessed, because you have obeyed My voice."

Before Abraham died he saw how God carried out this promise. He secured for Isaac a wife from among his relatives. Her name was Rebekah. Although God blessed him, he had no children. He prayed to God, and God heard his prayer.

Isaac blesses Jacob instead of Esau, his first-born son.

7. JACOB AND ESAU

ISAAC and Rebekah had twin sons named Jacob and Esau. Esau, the first-born, was his father's favorite because he was a hunter, rough and hairy; whereas the mother loved Jacob, who was a quiet man who lived in tents.

Jacob was cooking some lentil soup one day when Esau came in tired and hungry. "Give me some soup, I beg of you," he said.

"I will," said Jacob, "if you will sell me your right to be called the eldest son." So Esau agreed, and sold his birthright for a bowl of lentil soup. In this way, Jacob bought the right to his brother's place.

Now when Isaac was old and his eyes were dim so that he could not see, he called Esau to him and said, "My son, take your bow and arrows and go out to the field and get me some game and prepare for me some meat that I like. Bring it to me that I may eat, and that I may give you my blessing before I die."

Esau went out to the field to hunt, and while he was gone, Rebekah prepared a dish for Isaac from the meat of two young goats. She said to Jacob, "Take this to your father, and he will give you his blessing."

But Jacob said, "Esau, my brother, is a hairy man and I am not. My father may feel me and I shall be like a deceiver, and he will not bless me."

"Obey me, my son," said Rebekah, and she put Esau's best clothes on Jacob and covered his hands and neck with the skins of goats.

So Jacob brought in the meat to Isaac and said, "Father, this is your first-born, Esau, with the game you wanted. Now give me your blessing."

But Isaac said, "How did you find it so quickly, my son?"

"Because the Lord sent it," said Jacob.

Then Isaac felt his son and said, "The voice is Jacob's but the hands are the hands of Esau. Are you truly my son Esau?"

And Jacob said, "I am."

"Bring me the meat," said Isaac, "and kiss me, my son." And he gave him his blessing. As soon as Isaac had finished blessing Jacob, Esau came in from the hunt.

When Esau found that Jacob had taken away his blessing, he was very angry and he wanted to kill him.

The mother warned Jacob, "Your brother will kill you if you stay here. Go at once to Laban, my brother, and stay until Esau forgets his anger." So Jacob started his journey toward his uncle's house.

Jacob and his family would enjoy God's blessing and have Canaan as their home. They also would have the duty of carrying on the promise of the Messiah.

*Out of jealousy, Joseph's brothers sell him to Egyptian
merchants for twenty pieces of silver.*

8. JOSEPH AND HIS BROTHERS

JACOB'S favorite son was Joseph. To show his love for Joseph, Jacob gave him a coat of many colors. This made the other brothers very jealous of Joseph.

When Joseph was sixteen years old, he had a dream. He told his brothers that he had dreamed that they were harvesting in the field, and that all their sheaves of wheat came and bowed down to his sheaf.

His brothers said, "Shall you be ruler over us?" And they hated him still more.

Joseph had another dream in which he saw the sun, the moon, and eleven stars bow down before him and honor him.

One day as the brothers were pasturing their father's sheep, they saw Joseph coming across the field. "Here comes the dreamer," they said to one another. "Let us kill him, and see what becomes of his dreams!"

Out of jealousy they planned to kill him. But Reuben, the oldest, wishing to save Joseph's life, said, "Let us not kill him, but throw him into a pit." So they took off his coat of many colors and threw him into a pit.

Judah, one of the brothers, happened to see a caravan passing by on the way to Egypt; and he said, "What good will it do us to kill our brother? Let us sell him to these merchants instead!"

The others agreed. So they lifted Joseph up out of the pit and sold him to the merchants for twenty pieces of silver. The merchants took Joseph to Egypt.

Then the brothers killed a young goat. They dipped Joseph's coat in the blood and took it to their father. "See what we have found," they said. "Is this Joseph's coat?"

"It is my son's coat! Some wild beast has torn him to pieces," cried the father. And weeping and mourning for his son, he refused to be consoled.

Joseph sold by his brothers is like Jesus Christ who was sold by Judas, one of His apostles, for thirty pieces of silver.

Joseph refuses to do wrong in order to please Potiphar's wife.

9. JOSEPH IN POTIPHAR'S HOUSE

WHEN the merchants, who had bought Joseph, arrived in Egypt, they sold him to Potiphar, a captain in the king's army.

The Lord was with Joseph. The master saw that the Lord gave success to everything that was put into Joseph's hand. So Potiphar gave him full charge over his household.

But Potiphar's wife, who at first was very friendly to Joseph, afterward became his enemy, because Joseph would not do wrong to please her. She told her husband falsely that Joseph had done a wicked deed. Her husband believed her, became very angry at Joseph, and threw him in prison.

One night, King Pharaoh himself had a dream—really two dreams. And in the morning he sent for all the wise men of Egypt and told them his dreams; but no one could give the meaning of them. The king was troubled, for he felt that the dreams had some meaning, which it was important for him to know.

Then suddenly the chief butler, who was by the king's table, remembered that Joseph had told him the exact meaning of a dream he had two years before, and he said, "I remember a young Hebrew in the prison who explained a dream for me; and all that he said came true."

King Pharaoh sent to the prison for Joseph. Joseph was taken out, was dressed in new garments, and was led in to Pharaoh in the palace.

Then the king told his dreams. "Joseph, I have dreamed that I saw seven fat cows grazing in a meadow beside the river; and seven thin cows came and ate them up. But afterward the thin cows were just as thin as ever. And I saw seven good full ears of corn that were eaten by seven dry ears."

Joseph said, "God will help me explain the king's dreams. The two dreams are one. God has shown the king what He is about to do. The seven fat cows are seven years of plenty. The seven good ears of corn are those same seven years of plenty. The seven thin cows are seven years of famine. The seven thin ears are those same seven years of famine. Let the king choose a wise man to rule over Egypt. Let this ruler gather corn during the years of plenty, so that the people may have food during the seven years of famine."

The king heard all that Joseph said and was pleased. He said, "Since God has shown you all this, there is no other man as wise as you. I will appoint you to do this work and to rule over the land of Egypt. All the people shall be under you; only on the throne of Egypt, will I be above you."

Then Pharaoh, took from his own hand the ring which held his seal, and put it on Joseph's hand, so that he could sign for the king and seal in the king's place. He made Joseph ride in a chariot which was next in rank to his own. And thus Joseph was ruler over all the land of Egypt.

Joseph makes himself known to his brothers who have come seeking grain.

10.   JOSEPH'S GREATNESS

FOR seven years there were rich harvests in Egypt, and Joseph stored up grain every year. So, when seven years of famine came, there was food for the Egyptians and food to sell to the people of other lands. It was Joseph who had charge of selling the grain to those who came, driven by famine, from every country on earth.

The king said to the people, "Go to Joseph. Do whatever he commands."

There came to Joseph ten men from Canaan, who bent very low before him. He remembered how they had bowed down to him in his boyhood dreams.

But he cast one of them, Simeon, into prison. Then he gave them as much grain as they could carry, saying, "Bring Benjamin to see me, and I will set Simeon free."

Soon the corn that the brothers had bought was gone. When Judah, one of the brothers, promised to bring back Benjamin, Jacob agreed to let his youngest son go. The brothers set out for Egypt.

When Joseph saw Benjamin, he wept for joy. He made a banquet for his brothers and ordered that their sacks should be filled with grain. But his steward was to put Joseph's own silver cup into the sack that belonged to Benjamin.

As planned by Joseph, the cup was found in Benjamin's sack, and the brothers had to return to Joseph's house. Then Joseph said, "Let Benjamin remain as my servant. The rest of you may return home."

Judah cried, "Take me as your servant! What shall I say to my father if Benjamin does not return? Jacob will die of grief."

At these words Joseph began to weep before them and said, "I am Joseph your brother."

Then all the brothers were very happy.

When Jacob heard that Joseph was ruler of Egypt, he could not at first believe it. Then he said, "Joseph is alive; I will go and see him before I die."

So Jacob set out on his journey with all that he had. Joseph got into his chariot and went to meet his father on the way. He embraced him, kissed him, and wept with joy.

Joseph gave his father and his brothers rich land in Goshen.

The daughter of Pharaoh finds Moses among the reeds at the river's edge.

11. MOSES, PRINCE AND LEADER

AFTER many years a new king ruled Egypt. He was afraid of the Israelites, because they had become very numerous and powerful; so he put them to hard labor and made slaves of them. Then he commanded that every newborn Israelite boy should be thrown into the Nile.

Just at this time Moses was born, and his mother hid him as long as she could, for he was a beautiful child. But when he was three months old, she laid him in a little cradle and set it among the bushes at the river's edge. His sister stood a little way off, to see what would become of him.

Soon the daughter of Pharaoh came down with her maids to bathe in the river. When she saw the cradle among the reeds, she sent a maid to get it. The baby started to cry, and the heart of the princess was touched.

Then his sister ran up and asked, "Shall I get a Hebrew nurse for the baby?"

"Yes, do so," said Pharaoh's daughter. The girl went and called the child's mother.

"Nurse this child for me," said Pharaoh's daughter, "and I will pay you." The mother nursed him and brought him up. And the child grew and Pharaoh's daughter took him as her own son. She called him "Moses," for she said, "I drew him out of the water."

Moses was looked upon as a member of Pharaoh's household. He grew up like a prince and studied with the other children at the court of Pharaoh. He learned to read and write while his people were living in slavery.

But Moses did not forget that he was an Israelite. He sorrowed when he saw his people suffer. One day, when he was a young man, he saw an Egyptian master striking an Israelite. Moses was angry. He struck the Egyptian and killed him.

The next day Moses learned that his deed was known. He was afraid. Pharaoh wanted to put Moses to death. But Moses fled from Egypt into another country.

One day Moses defended the daughters of a priest of that country. Later, Moses married one of these women and became a shepherd for his father-in-law.

The king of Egypt died. The Israelites called on God to rescue them. Remembering His promise to their fathers — Abraham, Isaac and Jacob — God heard their prayer. He made ready to deliver them from their trials.

God speaks to Moses from the burning bush.

12. THE BURNING BUSH

ONE day Moses, while leading the sheep of his father-in-law near a mountain, was startled by the sight of a bush on fire. He wondered why it did not burn up. He came closer to look at it, and he heard his name called by the voice of God. The voice told Moses to take off his sandals, for the place was holy.

From the bush God spoke to Moses: "I have heard the prayers of the Children of Israel. I have seen how they suffer at the hands of the Egyptians. I will deliver them from their masters, and take them to a land flowing with milk and honey. Go to the king of Egypt, and ask him to let the Israelites go to the desert to offer sacrifice."

Then God said to Moses, "Tell them that **He who Is** has sent you." This is the name by which the Israelites since that time have known God. This name meant the everlasting and faithful God.

Moses was still afraid to go back into Egypt. He made excuses. He said he was not good at talking. So God promised him his brother Aaron to speak for him and to help him. Moses next told how powerful the Egyptian king was. But God said to Moses that he would have powers greater than those of Pharaoh.

Moses and Aaron went to ask the king of Egypt, in the name of the Lord, to let the Israelites go to sacrifice in the desert.

The king answered, "Who is the Lord, that I should hear His voice? I do not know Him. I will not let the Israelites go."

At God's command Moses and Aaron again went to the king. They asked him to let the Israelites go. Aaron threw his staff on the floor to show the power of God, and the staff became a serpent. The king's magicians also cast their staffs down, and their staffs also turned into serpents. But Aaron's staff ate up all the other staffs. Still the king would not free the Children of Israel.

The Angel of Death passes over the houses of the Israelites, who celebrate the First Passover, and does not kill their first-born.

13. THE PLAGUES OF EGYPT

BECAUSE the king of Egypt would not free the Children of Israel, God punished the land of Egypt. Every time that the king refused Moses, God sent the Egyptians a new plague. In all He sent ten plagues.

First, the water in the river turned to blood. Second, frogs in great numbers filled the land. Third, the dust was changed into small insects that covered everything. Fourth, there came a pest of flies. Fifth, a disease killed all the cattle. Sixth, boils broke out on man and beast. Seventh, hail and lightning came. Eighth, locusts ate up what the hail had left. Ninth, darkness covered Egypt. Still the king would not let the Israelites go.

Finally, God said to Moses, "I will bring one more plague upon the Egyptians, one that will force the king to free My people. Every first-born in Egypt shall die, from the first-born of Pharaoh himself to that of the slaves. There will be great weeping in Egypt."

Before this last evil came upon Egypt, God ordered the Israelites to prepare for their escape. They were to offer a special sacrifice. On the tenth day of the month, each family was to take a lamb. They were to keep the lamb until the fourteenth day of the month. In the evening they were to offer it in sacrifice and sprinkle their doorposts with its blood. Then they were to roast the lamb and eat it with unleavened bread and lettuce.

At midnight the Angel of Death passed through Egypt, killing all the first-born of the Egyptians—from the first-born of the king to the first-born of the poorest Egyptian—and taking also the first-born of all animals.

Among the Israelites no one died. The Angel of Death spared them when he saw the blood of the lamb which God had commanded them to sprinkle on the doorposts. This was the first Passover, or Pasch.

In fear the king sent for Moses and Aaron during the night. "Go," said he. "Take your flocks and your people. Leave Egypt."

The waters divide and the Israelites cross the Red Sea on dry ground.

14. THE CROSSING OF THE RED SEA

MOSES led the Israelites out of Egypt. There went out in that night six hundred thousand men, descended from the seventy who came into Egypt with their father Jacob. With all their goods they set out for the Promised Land.

God, going before them in a cloud by day, and a pillar of fire by night, led them toward the desert and the Red Sea.

But when Pharaoh and his men saw that the Israelites were gone, they said to themselves, "What have we done! We have freed our slaves!"

Pharaoh took his chariots and horsemen and went after the Israelites. When they saw this great army coming after them, the Israelites were afraid. They blamed Moses, crying to him, "Why did you bring us out of Egypt to die in this desert?"

Moses answered, "God will protect us."

The pillar of cloud that had gone before the Israelites to show them the way went behind them and hid them from the Egyptians.

Behind them came an army against which they could not hope to fight. Before them stretched the sea. But Moses knew that God was with him. He prayed for help. Then God told Moses to stretch forth his staff over the sea. Moses did this. A strong and burning wind blew all through the night. In the morning the waters were divided. There was a dry path where before there had been only water. That the people would not be afraid, an angel went before them. The Israelites crossed the Red Sea on dry ground.

Then the Egyptians went in after them, horsemen, chariots, horses, and all. With great speed they dashed along the path through the sea. They even reached its center. But the sand became soft again. Their chariot wheels were fastened in it. All became frightened.

The Lord then said to Moses, "Lift up your hand and bring the water back again." And the water came rushing back and covered the horses and the chariots and the men, till there was not so much as one of them left.

God rains food from heaven on Moses and the starving Israelites.

15. THE MANNA IN THE DESERT

THE Israelites set out across the desert. But they kept saying, "If only we had died in Egypt, instead of starving here! Now who will give us any meat in this desert?"

The Lord said to Moses, "I will rain food from heaven for you. And you shall know that I am the Lord your God." That very evening many birds came. The people caught them and ate.

The next morning when the people looked out of their tents, they saw all around the camp, on the sand, little white flakes, like snow or frost. Since they had never seen anything like this before, they said, "What is it?" In the language of the Israelites, the Hebrew language, "What is it?" is the word "Manhu." From then on this new thing was given the name "Manna."

And Moses said to them, "This is the bread which the Lord has given you to eat. Go out and gather it, as much as you need. But take only as much as you need for today, for it will not keep; and God will give you more tomorrow."

So the people went out and gathered the manna. The taste of it was like bread made with honey.

When some of the people tried to keep the manna until the next day, it spoiled during the night. So each morning they took up just enough of the manna for that day. On the sixth day they gathered twice as much, to provide for the Sabbath, and it did not spoil. On the seventh day manna did not fall. In this way God showed that His day must be kept holy.

God sent the Israelites manna for forty years in the desert, until they came to the Promised Land. Manna is like the Eucharistic Bread, the Body and Blood of our Lord, which comes from heaven to feed our souls during our life on earth, till we come at last to heaven, our eternal home, the land of promise.

Seeing the golden calf, Moses breaks the tablets of the Commandments at the foot of Mount Sinai.

16. THE TEN COMMANDMENTS

MOSES brought the people out from the camp to the foot of Mount Sinai. In the morning of the third day there was thunder and lightning. All the mountain shook and gave out smoke like a furnace. A trumpet sounded loudly. God began to speak from the cloud.

Then God called Moses up to the top of Mount Sinai and gave him Commandments written on tablets of stone. God spoke and said:

"I, the Lord, am your God. You shall not have other gods besides Me.

"You shall not take the name of the Lord, your God, in vain.

"Remember to keep holy the sabbath day.

"Honor your father and your mother.

"You shall not kill.

"You shall not commit adultery.

"You shall not steal.

"You shall not bear false witness against your neighbor.

"You shall not covet your neighbor's wife.

"You shall not covet anything that belongs to your neighbor."

Moses was with the Lord forty days and forty nights. The people became tired waiting for him. They went to Aaron and said, "Make us gods to worship."

Then Aaron said, "Bring your gold ornaments to me." He melted the gold, and from the metal he shaped an image of a calf.

Moses prayed God to spare the people. When he came down the mountainside, and saw the golden calf, and the people singing and dancing around it, he was angry. He threw down the tablets of stone and broke them at the foot of the mountain. The golden calf he burned and ground into powder.

Again Moses went up Mount Sinai, to pray for the people. God told him to make two tablets of stone like the ones he had broken. Moses wrote the Ten Commandments on them.

*Moses strikes the rock with the staff and water gushes forth
for the people and for all their cattle.*

17. MIRACLES IN THE DESERT

THE Israelites again came to a region where there was no water, and they called to Moses, "Why have you brought us to such a place? There is not even any water to drink."

Then Moses and Aaron threw themselves down in front of the Lord's tent.

The Lord said to Moses, "Take your staff in your hand, and call the people together. Then strike the rock, and it will give water for them."

Moses called the people together in front of the rock. Then he took his staff in his hand and said to the people, "Hear, you rebels! Must we draw water for you out of this rock?"

Twice he struck the rock with his staff; and water gushed out, for the people and for all their cattle.

Now Moses had struck the rock twice, because he knew how wicked the Israelites had been. He had wondered if God would give them water, as He had promised. When God saw the anger of Moses and his lack of faith, He said to him, "Because you have not believed Me, you shall not lead the people into the land which I will give them."

Again the Children of Israel were very ungrateful to God in the desert, even though He had been so good to them. They even complained against God.

To punish the wicked Israelites, God sent serpents to bite them. Many died. The people begged Moses to pray God that the serpents be taken away. Then God said to Moses, "Make a serpent of bronze. Everyone who looks on it shall live."

Moses made a serpent of bronze and set it up for a sign. When someone was bitten by a serpent, he would look at the bronze serpent and be cured.

This serpent of bronze is like Jesus, who was nailed on the cross of Calvary to save mankind.

Rahab hides the two Israelite spies under stalks of flax.

18. RAHAB AND THE TWO SPIES

AFTER wandering in the desert forty years, the people of Israel reached the river Jordan, at the doorway of the Promised Land. Moses called the people together and told them that it was God's command that Joshua should take his place as their leader.

Then God took Moses up to the peak of Mount Nebo, showed him the country far and wide, and said, "That is the land I will give to the Children of Israel, but you shall not enter it, because you doubted Me."

Moses died at the age of one hundred and twenty years. He was a wise ruler and a great prophet. He wrote the first five books of the Bible.

God said to Joshua, "Arise and lead the people into the Promised Land. As I was with Moses, so I shall be with you. I will never forsake you. Take courage and be strong."

Joshua chose two careful men who were both brave and wise, and said to them, "Go across the river and get into the city of Jericho; find out all you can about it and come back in two days."

But they were seen going into a house which stood on the wall of the city, where a woman named Rahab lived. She hid the men on the roof of the house and heaped over them stalks of flax. The king of Jericho sent men to take them prisoners. But the officers could not find them.

Then the two men, at night, slid down a scarlet rope, which was later to hang in Rahab's window as a sign that her family would be spared. The two men told Joshua, "Truly the Lord has given to us all the land; for all the people in it are afraid of us, and will not dare to fight us."

The Ark of the Covenant was a chest of gold, in which were kept the two stone tablets of the Ten Commandments. It was also the sign of God's presence with His children. When the priests who carried the Ark came to the edge of the Jordan, the water divided, and all the people went across on dry land into the Promised Land.

*The priests blow the trumpets, the people shout, and the walls
of Jericho fall down.*

19. THE TAKING OF JERICHO

WHEN the people of Jericho heard how the Israelites had crossed the Jordan, they were very much afraid. They closed all the gates in the city walls.

At dawn, on the seventh day, the Israelites went up and marched around the city seven times to the sound of trumpets. But the seventh time, when the priests blew the trumpets, Joshua said to the people, "Shout! for the Lord has given you the city." The people gave such a mighty shout that the walls of Jericho fell down flat; and the Israelites went in and took the city.

Joshua said to the two spies, "Go and bring out Rahab and her family, and take them to a safe place."

After this Rahab was taken among the people of Israel, and one of the nobles of the tribe of Judah took her for his wife. From her line of descendants, many years after this, was born David the king. She was saved and blessed, because she had faith in the God of Israel.

The Israelite army climbed up over the ruined walls. The people in the city were wild with fear. They were either slain or taken prisoners by the Israelites.

Joshua said to his soldiers, "Nothing in this city belongs to you. It is the Lord's and is to be destroyed as an offering to the Lord."

So they brought together all the gold and precious things, and all that was in the houses. They took nothing for themselves. Whatever they found in the city they burned. They left the city of Jericho nothing but a waste.

Joshua did everything he could to make the people love God. He told them that God wanted them to conquer the land of Canaan because its people worshiped false gods. But the Israelites made friends with the Canaanites and even married them. Soon many of the Children of Israel forgot God and again began to worship idols.

*Joshua commands the sun to stand still and in this way
he defeats the Canaanites.*

20. JOSHUA CONQUERS THE LAND
OF CANAAN

A GROUP of five kings in the south of Canaan fought the Israelites before the walls of Gibeon, and Joshua was the victor. Joshua did not give his enemies time to form a line, but fell upon them so suddenly that they were confused, and fled before the men of Israel. Joshua followed his enemies as they fled and killed many of them. In their flight, the kings were overtaken by a hail storm. The stones were so large that many soldiers were killed by them. At this time Joshua prayed to the Lord to give him time to finish his victory. God allowed the light of day to remain longer than usual. It seemed as if the sun and moon stood still. In this way Joshua defeated the Canaanites.

This battle was very important, for on that day the land was won by the people of the Lord. If Israel had been defeated instead of Canaan, then the worship of the true God would have been stopped, and the world might have worshiped idols.

After this victory Joshua turned to the north, and led his army by a swift march against the kings who had united there to fight the Israelites. As suddenly as before, he fell upon these kings and their armies and won another great victory. Everywhere the tribes of Canaan were made to obey the Israelites, until all the mountain country was under Joshua's rule.

The Children of Israel were divided into twelve tribes, each tribe being named after one of Jacob's sons. The chief tribe was that of Judah, from which the Savior was to come, according to the prophecies.

Joshua divided Canaan among the tribes of Israel. Only the tribe of Levi, which was that of the priests, was not given any land. The priests were allowed to live among the other tribes and were to be supported by them.

Joshua had finished the work for which God had chosen him. He died at the age of one hundred and ten years.

*Boaz inquires about Ruth who is gathering grain in his fields,
and arranges for her to find more grain than usual.*

21. THE DEVOTION OF RUTH

THROUGH the Judges, God saved His people and kept His religion alive among them. At that time there was a famine in Palestine. A man of Judah, called Elimelech, went with his wife, Naomi, into Moab to live. Soon after, this man took sick and died. There his two sons married Moabite women, whose names were Orpah and Ruth. The two sons also died.

Naomi was left alone with her two daughters-in-law. Hearing that there was food again at home, Naomi decided to return to Judah, her own country. Orpah went back to her people in Moab. But Ruth was devoted to Naomi and said: "Where you go, I will go; where you stay, I will stay; your people shall be my people, and your God, my God."

Ruth and Naomi returned to Judah and settled down at Bethlehem. They were very poor. At the time of the barley harvest Ruth went to the field of a man named Boaz to gather the grain left over by the harvesters. Only in this way could she and Naomi have food.

When Boaz heard about her, he arranged that she would find more grain than usual. He soon fell in love with the young widow.

Boaz was a relative of Ruth's husband. At that time there was a law of the Israelites by which the nearest relative of a man that died without having children should marry the widow. In this way Boaz took Ruth as his wife.

Their son, Obed, was the grandfather of David. Ruth was, therefore, a mother in the family from which our Savior was born. In this way God rewarded the devotion of Ruth.

Samson kills a lion with his great strength..

22. THE STRENGTH OF SAMSON

THE Philistines were a strong and warlike people who worshiped an idol called Dagon. And as before, the Israelites in their trouble cried to the Lord. God sent them Samson, who was known for his great strength.

Samson married Dalilah, a Philistine woman. The Philistines offered to give her money if she would find out what made him so strong and how they could overcome him.

Once Samson met a young lion that was raging and roaring. In his strength he tore the lion apart as he would a lamb.

Dalilah begged Samson to reveal his secret to her, but he refused. One day, in a weak moment, he said, "A razor has never passed over my head, for I am consecrated to God. If my head should be shaved, my strength would leave me."

When Samson was asleep, Dalilah had his seven locks cut off. He had broken his vow to the Lord, and the Lord had left him. He was now as weak as other men.

The Philistines captured Samson and put out his eyes. Then they threw him into prison where all day he had to work grinding grain. While working, he allowed his hair to grow again. This was a sign that he had again consecrated himself to God.

Samson pulls down the pillars of the temple.

One day, three thousand Philistines were feasting in their temple. They led Samson in that they might make fun of him. Samson said to the little boy who led him, "Let me touch the pillars which support the whole house, and let me lean against them, to rest myself a little."

Then he prayed, "O Lord God, restore to me my former strength!" He placed one arm around the pillar on one side and the other arm around the pillar on the other side, and he said, "Let me die with the Philistines."

And bowing forward with all his might and pulling the pillars over with him, he brought down the roof upon those who were under it. Samson himself was among the dead; but he died performing his duty for God.

*Hannah brings Samuel to Eli to set him apart for the
service of the Lord.*

23. THE CHILD SAMUEL

ELKANAH and Hannah lived in the hill country north of
Jerusalem. They had no children. Hannah went to pray
to the Lord, "Give me a son, and I will pledge him to
Your service all the days of his life."

This prayer was answered, for Hannah had a son and called
him "Samuel," meaning "Asked of the Lord." As soon as he
was old enough to leave his mother, she took her son and
went to the house of the Lord.

"This is the child the Lord has sent in answer to my
prayer," she said to Eli, the priest. "He is to be set apart
for the service of God all the days of his life."

So the child Samuel lived at the Temple, helping Eli in
the priestly duties. And every year when his family came to
worship, his mother brought him a little coat which she had
made for him.

One night after Eli had gone to bed, while the light was still burning in the Temple, Samuel was lying awake. Suddenly he heard someone calling, "Samuel!"

The boy answered, "Here I am," and ran to Eli, saying, "Here I am, for you called me."

"I did not call, my son," he said; "go back to sleep."

Samuel went and lay down; but a second time he heard the call, "Samuel!"

He jumped up and went to Eli, saying, "Here I am, for you called me."

This happened three times. At last Eli saw that God had called the child, and he said to him, "Go, lie down, and if you hear the voice again, you shall say, 'Speak, Lord, for Your servant is listening.'"

Samuel went back to sleep. After a while he once more heard a voice calling him. He answered, "Speak, Lord, for Your servant is listening."

Then God told him that for their sins Eli and his sons would no longer be leaders of the Children of Israel. Samuel was to take their place.

The Israelites were badly defeated by the Philistines. The Ark was captured and Eli's sons were killed. By this time Eli was an old man. When the sad news was brought back to him, he died of the shock. In this way Samuel became the leader of God's people.

After many evils had come upon them, the Philistines sent the Ark back to the Children of Israel. Samuel told the people to cast away the idols they had been serving because they were the cause of their suffering. The people obeyed and promised to serve God as they should. This faithful service of God, and the hope they had in His promises, brought the Chosen People still closer together. They began to have power against the Philistines, and there was peace again. As Judge, Samuel went each year to different cities to offer sacrifice and to govern the people.

Samuel tells the people that God has chosen Saul as their king.

24. KING SAUL

THE elders of all the tribes of Israel came to Samuel at his home in Ramah, and they said to him, "You are growing old, and your sons do not rule as well as you have ruled. All the lands around us have kings. Let us have a king also. You choose a king for us."

Samuel prayed to the Lord, and the Lord said to him, "Listen to the people in what they ask. Choose a king for them."

Then Samuel sent the people to their homes and promised to find a king for them.

There was in the tribe of Benjamin a young man named Saul. He was a very tall man and noble-looking. He was taller than any other man in Israel.

The Lord spoke to Samuel and said, "Tomorrow I will send you a man out of the tribe of Benjamin, and you shall make him the prince of My people, and he shall save My people from the Philistines."

Saul went out with a servant to find Samuel. When Samuel saw this tall young man coming to meet him, he heard the Lord's voice saying, "This is the man of whom I spoke to you. He is the one that shall rule over My people."

That night Saul and his servant slept in the best room of Samuel's house. The next morning Samuel brought out oil and poured it on Saul's head and said, "God has anointed you king of the Israelites. You shall rule over them and protect them from their enemies."

Samuel called all the people and told them that God had chosen a king for them. They were happy when they saw Saul. And Samuel said, "Look at the man whom the Lord has chosen! There is not another like him among all the people."

And all the people shouted, "God save the king! Long live the king!"

So after two hundred years under the sixteen Judges, Israel now had a king.

Samuel tells Saul that God will take away his kingdom because of his disobedience.

25. SAUL DISOBEYS GOD

THE Children of Israel who lived on the other side of the Jordan were suffering from the Ammonites. They sent messengers to Saul telling him of their danger. At once Saul called together men from the other tribes. With this army he marched against the Ammonites and defeated them.

At another time, Samuel told Saul, "Do not march until I come to offer a sacrifice and to call upon God."

Saul, at the head of his forces, waited for the arrival of Samuel who was slow in coming. Finally Saul, impatient to be off, offered a sacrifice. When Samuel came, he was angry at Saul. Saul had no right to offer a sacrifice, because he was not a priest.

"You have done wrong," said Samuel. "You have not kept God's commands. If you had obeyed and trusted the Lord, He would have kept you safe. But now God will find some other man who will do His will, a man after His own Heart, and God will in His own time take the kingdom from you and give it to him."

One time Saul was sent by God against a people who lived to the south of the Promised Land. He was told to destroy them and all they owned because they had offended God by their worship of idols. When Saul came to their city, he won a great victory. But he did not do as he was told. He spared the king and his people. He kept for himself and his soldiers the best of the flocks and all that was beautiful. This was a sin of disobedience.

Again Samuel came to Saul and said to him, "To obey is better than to offer sacrifice. To disobey God's word is as evil as to worship idols. You have refused to obey the voice of the Lord, and the Lord will take away your kingdom from you."

After this there came over Saul a great change. His sin of disobedience brought upon him the anger of God. God took from him the courage which had made him strong. Instead, he was troubled by an evil temper that was with him at all times.

Saul attempts to kill David with a spear.

26. DAVID AND SAUL

THE prophet Samuel was in Bethlehem, at God's command, to choose a king for Israel from among the sons of Jesse.

Jesse called each of his sons to stand before Samuel, yet of seven sons not one was chosen. And Samuel said to Jesse, "Are these all your sons?"

"There is still a young one," said Jesse, "but he is tending the sheep."

The father called for David, and David came in from the hillsides of Judah. He was a handsome boy. The Lord said to Samuel, "This is he. Anoint him."

So Samuel brought out oil and anointed him king of Israel in the presence of his brothers. This seemed strange, because there was already a king on the throne—Saul. Yet from that time on, the spirit of God came upon David, God's chosen king. Alone with his flocks under the wide sky, he played his harp and sang aloud for joy.

Saul was sad when he learned that God no longer wanted him to be king of Israel. One day Saul's servants said, "Let us bring you a man who will play on the harp and cheer you up. Then your sad thoughts will be driven away."

Then one of the servants said, "There is a fine player named David, a shepherd, strong and handsome. And the Lord is with him."

So Saul sent messengers to Jesse saying, "Send me David your son who is with the sheep."

David came to Saul. Saul loved him deeply and made him his armor-bearer. He did not know that Samuel had anointed David. After that, when the sadness came, David would take the harp and play so sweetly that Saul would forget his troubles.

David and Jonathan, Saul's son, became the best of friends. All the people grew to love David so much that at last Saul felt jealous. He made up his mind to kill David.

One day when David came to play on the harp, Saul threw his spear at him. Twice David avoided the spear, and then he fled into the night.

*The stone from David's sling strikes the giant Goliath
on the forehead and knocks him down.*

27. DAVID AND GOLIATH

ONCE the Philistines built their camp on one mountain; the Israelites pitched theirs on the opposite mountain.

Out of the Philistines' camp came a ten-foot giant named Goliath. He was covered with bronze armor. He called out to the Israelites, "Choose a man from among you. Let him come down to fight me. If he kills me, we will be your servants. If I kill him, then you shall become our servants."

Saul and the Israelites were very much afraid. Many days passed. Still no Israelite dared to fight Goliath. One day David arrived at the Israelite camp to see his three brothers who were in Saul's army. He heard the giant shouting, "I defy you, Israelites! Give me a man, so that we may fight together."

David asked, "Who is this man who defies the army of God? I will fight him!"

"You cannot fight Goliath," said Saul; "you are only a boy and he has fought many battles."

"I have killed both a lion and a bear that took a lamb of my father's flock. God, who protected me from those wild animals, will protect me against this Philistine giant," answered David.

So David took his shepherd's staff and his sling in his hand, and picked out five smooth stones from the brook and went to meet Goliath.

The giant came forward to meet his enemy. A shield-bearer marched in front of him. When he saw coming toward him only a boy, the giant was angry and roared, "Am I a dog that you come to me with a staff? Come, and I will feed you to the birds!"

And David said, "You come to me with a sword, a spear, and a shield. I come in the name of God, who will deliver you into my hands."

Then the boy took a stone and put it in his sling and shot it. The stone struck Goliath in the forehead and he fell to the ground. David took the giant's sword and cut off his head.

Then David was given a place of honor among the fighting men of Israel. And all the people loved David.

David spares Saul's life but takes his spear and water bottle.

28. DAVID LOVES SAUL

HEN David saw that Saul wanted to kill him, he fled into the wilderness. Saul said, "He shall surely die."

At one time David was hiding with a few men in a great cave near the Dead Sea. They were far back in the darkness of the cave, when they saw Saul come into the cave alone and lie down to sleep. David's men whispered to him, "Now is the time of which the Lord said, 'I will give your enemy into your hands, and you may do to him whatever you please.'"

Then David went toward Saul very quietly with his sword in his hand. His men thought he would kill Saul, but instead, he only cut off a part of Saul's long robe.

As Saul left the cave, David called out from a distance, "My lord the king! See this piece of your robe I have cut off? Could I not have killed you? Truly I will not lay my hand on you."

Not long afterwards Saul was again seeking David in the wilderness of Judah with three thousand men. From his hiding place in the mountains David looked down on the plain and saw Saul's camp. That night David and one of his men descended quietly and walked into the middle of Saul's camp, while all his guards were asleep. Saul himself was sleeping, with his spear standing in the ground at his head, and a bottle of water near it.

David's follower knew that David would not kill King Saul, and he said to David, "God has given your enemy into your hand again. Let me strike him through to the ground at one stroke—only once; I will not need to strike twice."

But David said, "You shall not destroy him. Who can strike the anointed of the Lord without being guilty of a crime? Let the Lord strike him, or let him die when God wills it, but he shall not die by my hand. Let us take his spear and his water bottle, and let us go."

They walked out of the camp without awakening anyone. In the morning David called out to Saul's men, "Why have you not kept watch over your king? See, here is the king's spear and his bottle of water!"

Saul kills himself with his own sword when he sees that
he is defeated in battle.

29. SAUL'S DEATH

KING Saul was old and weakened by disease and trouble. The Lord had forsaken him. The Philistines climbed up Mount Gilboa and fell upon the Israelites in their camp. Many of the men of Israel were slain in the fight, and many more fled. Saul's three sons, one of them the brave and noble Jonathan, were killed.

When Saul saw that the battle had gone against him, that his sons were slain, and that his enemies were pressing closely upon him, he called his armor-bearer and said, "Draw your sword and kill me; it would be better for me to die by your hand than for the Philistines to come upon me and kill me."

But the armor-bearer would not draw his sword against his king, the Lord's anointed. Then Saul took his own sword and fell upon it and killed himself among the bodies of his own men.

On the next day the Philistines came and took off Saul's armor and sent it to the temple of their idol, Dagon. They fastened the bodies of Saul and his three sons to the wall of a Canaanite city. Some men of Jabesh, a city which Saul rescued, rose up in the night and took down from the wall the bodies of Saul and his sons and carried them to Jabesh. That they might not be taken away again, they burned them and buried their ashes under a tree. They mourned Saul seven days. Thus came to an end Saul's reign of forty years, which began well, but ended in ruin because he forsook the Lord God of Israel.

After their victory over Saul, the Philistines were masters of the Children of Israel. The men of Israel left their villages and fled, and the Philistines came and lived in the villages. They made the people suffer greatly.

At this time David again asked the Lord what he should do. God told him to go up to Hebron, one of the larger cities of Judah. There the men of Judah made him their king. David was a wise ruler.

The Ark is carried into Jerusalem with David at the head of the procession, dancing with joy before the ark.

30. THE CITY OF DAVID

THE first thing that David did as king was to lead his soldiers against the city of Jerusalem. He conquered it and made it his capital. He built a wall around it and called it the City of David.

During the time that he ruled, David tried to lead the people to worship God as they should. He brought to Jerusalem the Ark that had been captured by the Philistines. He built a Tabernacle on Mount Zion to house the Ark. Each day sacrifices were offered before the Ark.

The Ark was carried into the city with shouting and dancing, and with the sound of the trumpets and harps and flutes. Thirty thousand armed men were the guard of honor, and very many people joined in the great procession. David himself, playing on his harp and dancing with joy before the Ark, was in the procession.

David rebuilt the city, making new walls and towers and courts and palaces, so that Jerusalem in her beauty and safety became for the Children of Israel a holy place, a City of God. David divided the priests into twenty-four groups. Each group was to serve in turn before the Lord. He chose four thousand musicians to sing praises and to play music before God each day.

David was a good king to his people and protected them from their enemies. During his rule Israel became great and powerful. But David was also a great poet. Inspired by God, he wrote beautiful poems that today we call the Psalms. They are songs of praise and thanksgiving, and of sorrow for sin.

God loved David and promised, through the prophet Nathan, that the Savior would be born of his family. The promise said, "Your house shall be faithful, and your kingdom shall be forever. Your throne shall be firm forever." The Messiah was to be the King whose throne will be forever.

David wanted to build a Temple, but God by a prophet sent him a message, saying, "Not you, but your son shall build Me a Temple. I will set up his kingdom forever."

Absalom's thick hair is caught in the branches of a great oak tree.

31. THE DEATH OF ABSALOM

AVID had to suffer many trials as punishment for his sins. His greatest trial was the revolt of his son Absalom.

Now in all the country there was no one so handsome as the king's son Absalom. But Absalom wished to have his father's kingdom. With promises of rich reward he stole away the hearts of many people, and at last he raised an army against the king.

To avoid a battle with his son in Jerusalem, David left the city, and went barefoot and weeping up Mount Olivet. And all those who were with him wept as they went along. David became a wanderer in his old age.

In the woods of Ephraim the soldiers of Absalom fought against the soldiers of the king. David's last words to his men were, "Spare my boy Absalom!"

Absalom fled on his mule through the forest. As he was riding, he went under a great oak tree, and Absalom's thick hair caught in the branches; and while the mule dashed away, the rider was left hanging between earth and sky. There the king's soldiers found him and killed him.

A man came running with news of the battle. He called to the king, "All is well."

And the king asked, "Is the young man Absalom safe?"

When he learned that his son was dead, the king covered his face and cried aloud in bitter grief, "My son Absalom, would to God I had died for you. O Absalom, my son!"

Then the men of Judah brought David back again to Jerusalem. And in his faith he found comfort.

God rewarded David for his faithful service. During the closing years of David's life, peace had come to the kingdom. David gave more time to the services at the Tabernacle where the Ark of the Covenant was kept. In this way he showed his gratitude and devotion to God. After forty years as king of Israel, David died.

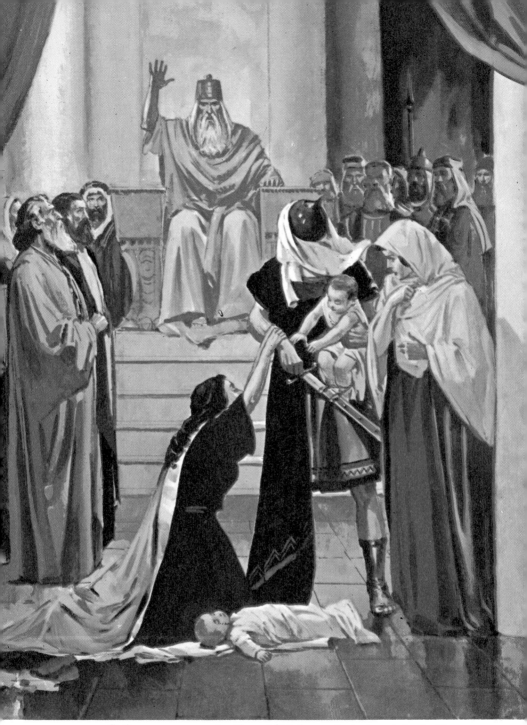

*Solomon prevents the child from being cut in half,
and gives it to its real mother.*

32. KING SOLOMON
(1015 B.C.)

DAVID laid up great treasures of gold and silver for the building of a Temple to the Lord, but God said to him, "You have been a man of war. My house shall be built by a man of peace. When you die, your son Solomon shall reign, and he shall have peace and shall build My house."

And Zadok, the priest, anointed the head of Solomon with holy oil and all the people cried aloud, "God save King Solomon!" From his deathbed David gave his last advice to his son.

One day two women came to Solomon. One of them said, "This woman and I were in the same house. Her child died at night. While I was asleep, she took my child and laid her dead child beside me."

The other woman answered, "That is not true. Your child is dead and mine is alive."

Then the king said, "Take a sword and cut the living child in half, and give half to one woman and half to the other."

But the woman whose child was alive said to the king, "I beg you, my lord, give her the child alive, and do not kill it."

The king said "Give the living child to this woman, for she is its mother."

The people saw that the wisdom of God was with King Solomon.

Solomon was not more than twenty years old when he became king and bore the heavy care of a great land. He had no wars, as David had before him, but at home and abroad his great kingdom was at peace as long as Solomon reigned.

Solomon begins to build God's Temple on Mount Moriah in Jerusalem.

33. THE TEMPLE OF SOLOMON

IN THE fourth year of his rule, Solomon began to build God's Temple on Mount Moriah in Jerusalem. The Temple was copied after the Tabernacle which was built before Mount Sinai in the desert, with its **Court, Holy Place,** and **Holy of Holies.** But the Temple was larger and was a house of stone and cedar, instead of a tent.

The Temple had two courts, both open to the sky, with walls of stone around them. The court in front was the **People's Court,** and beyond it was the **Court of the Priests.** At the east gate of this court stood the great altar of burnt offerings, built of rough stones. Near the altar stood a great brass tank for water.

Within the **Court of the Priests** stood the **Temple building,** made of marble and of cedar. It was a high tower in which were rooms for the high priest and his sons. Outside of **the Temple building** were rooms for the priests.

In back of **the Temple building** was the **Holy Place.** This was a long room in which stood the table for the twelve loaves of bread and golden altar of incense, and the golden lampstand.

Between the **Holy Place** and the **Holy of Holies** was a great veil. And in the **Holy of Holies** the priests placed the Ark of the Covenant. This was a chest of gold in which were kept the two stone tablets of the Ten Commandments. Into this room only the high priest was allowed to enter, and he only on one day in the year, the great Day of Atonement.

Seven years were spent in building the Temple. Then the Temple was dedicated and set apart for the worship of the Lord. Many offerings were burned upon the great altar. The Ark was brought from Mount Zion and placed in the **Holy of Holies,** and King Solomon knelt in front of the altar and offered a prayer to the Lord before all the people.

After many years, Solomon was led away from God by pagan women who were brought to his court. God was offended by Solomon's sins and punished him. While his son Rehoboam was king, ten tribes revolted and formed the kingdom of Israel.

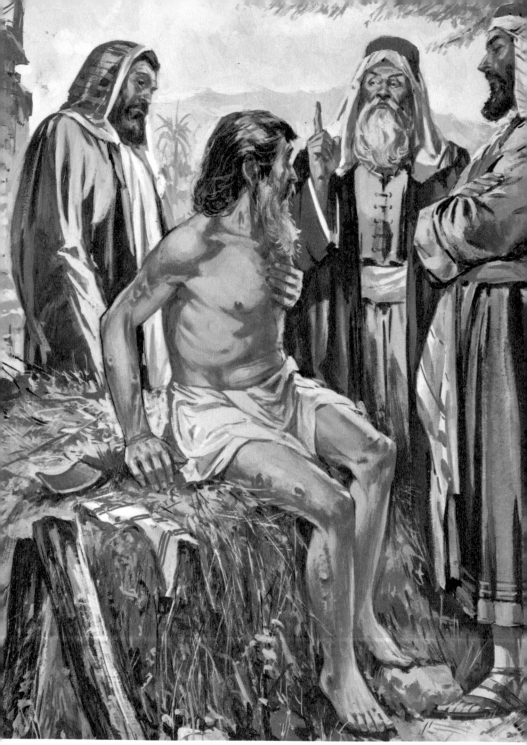

Job is filled with sorrow, but he blesses the Name of the Lord.

34. JOB'S PATIENCE

THERE lived in Arabia a very rich man named Job. He loved God and avoided sin. He had seven sons and three daughters. He had thousands of sheep and cattle.

One day God wished to prove the goodness of Job to Satan who said that it was easy for Job to be good because he was rich.

God said to Satan, "You can do what you want to Job's property, but do not hurt his body. You shall see how he will remain faithful to Me."

Soon after, a messenger arrived before Job to tell him that his cattle had been stolen and all his servants slain. Another messenger told him that his sheep and shepherds had been struck by lightning. A third messenger came to say that his camels and those who took care of them had been killed.

The fourth messenger brought the worst news: "There came a strong wind from the desert. It shook the whole house. The house fell and killed all your sons and daughters. I alone escaped to tell you."

When Job heard all this, he was filled with great sorrow. He did not sin by blaming God, but prayed, "The Lord gave, and the Lord has taken away! Blessed be the Name of the Lord!"

Satan caused sores to break out all over Job's body. But Job did not complain.

His friends said that his trials must be a punishment for his sins. But he answered that he had done no wrong. Job said, "Although He should kill me, I will trust in Him. He shall be my Savior. For I know that my Redeemer lives, and in the last day I shall rise out of the earth, and in my flesh I shall see my God."

God was much pleased with the patience of Job. He freed him from his sufferings. He gave him even more riches than he had had before. God also gave him seven sons and three daughters. Job lived happily till he was one hundred and forty years old.

*The false prophets pray in vain, while Elijah confidently
asks God to consume the sacrifice.*

35. THE PROPHET ELIJAH

THE Israelites often broke God's Commandments. They married pagans and even worshiped false gods. Out of pity for them, God sent holy men to lead them back to Him. These were the prophets. They also foretold the coming of the Savior. The greatest of the prophets were Elijah, Isaiah, and Jeremiah.

The prophet Elijah lived when King Ahab was ruling Israel. This king had married a pagan, Jezebel, and had built a temple to her god, Baal. Ahab also adored Baal.

Elijah was sent by God to warn Ahab. He said, "To punish you for worshiping idols, God will not send any rain for three years. There will be a famine."

With the country suffering from a great famine because there had been no rain for three years, God sent Elijah back to Ahab. He told the king that the famine was a punishment for his sins. The king's wife, Jezebel, had killed almost all the true prophets of God. In their place she had put several hundred false prophets to sing the praises of her false god. Elijah asked Ahab to gather these false prophets on Mount Carmel. The people also gathered there. Elijah said to them, "If the Lord is God, you should obey Him. But if the god of Jezebel is the true god, then follow him."

Elijah then asked for two oxen, one for the false prophets and one for himself. He said to these prophets, "You call upon your gods, and I will call upon the Lord. The god that shall answer by fire consuming the sacrifice will be known to be the true god." This plan seemed very good to the people.

The false prophets laid the ox upon an altar. They called upon their god from morning till noon, but there was no answer. They cried still louder and even cut themselves until they were covered with blood. But no answer came.

Then Elijah told the people to gather around him. He put wood on an altar and laid the ox on the wood. He poured buckets of water over the sacrifice. When the hour of the evening sacrifice came, Elijah prayed, "O Lord God of Abraham, Isaac, and Israel, show this day that You are the true God of Israel."

As he was praying, fire came down from heaven and burnt up the sacrifice and the altar itself. When the people saw this, they fell down to the ground and cried, "The Lord is God! The Lord is God!"

Elijah goes up in a whirlwind on the fiery chariot to heaven.

36. THE PROPHET ELISHA

GOD commanded Elijah to choose Elisha to take his place. Elisha, knowing that his master was about to leave him, went along with him to the river Jordan, about five miles. When they came to the bank of the Jordan, Elijah took his mantle and wrapped it together and struck the waters. Then the waters were divided on each side, and a path was made across the river; and the two prophets walked across on dry ground. And as they walked, Elijah said, "Ask what I may do for you before I am taken away from you."

Elisha answered him, "All that I ask is that your spirit shall come upon me in greater power than it comes upon any other man."

And Elijah said to him, "You have asked a great blessing; and if you see me when I am taken away, it shall come to you; but if you do not see me, it shall not come."

As they still went on and talked, suddenly a chariot of fire and horses of fire came between them and parted them; and Elijah went up in a whirlwind on the fiery chariot to heaven.

Elisha saw him going up toward heaven, and he cried out, "O my father, my father, the chariot of Israel, and the horsemen thereof!"

He meant that in losing Elijah the kingdom had lost more than an army of chariots and horsemen. After this he saw Elijah no more; but he caught up the mantle of Elijah which had fallen from him. With the mantle he struck the water of the Jordan which parted on either side, and Elisha walked across on dry ground.

The sons of the prophets saw Elisha walking through the river alone. They said, "The spirit of Elijah now rests upon Elisha," and they bowed down before him as their leader.

Elisha did wonderful things. He turned a bitter spring into sweet water in the city of Jericho, and he made poisoned food harmless. And once in a time of famine he satisfied the hunger of a hundred men with a few barley loaves and some fresh vegetables.

Jonah is cast forth by the whale.

37. THE PROPHET JONAH

GOD sent the prophet Jonah to preach to the people who lived in Nineveh in Assyria. They were enemies of the Israelites. Jonah did not want to go to Nineveh because he feared that if the Assyrians were converted, they might harm his people. Instead, he set out by boat for a far country. In this way he thought he could hide from God.

But God sent a violent storm upon the sea. "Throw me overboard," said Jonah to the sailors, "for I know that the storm has come because of me." So, praying to God for mercy, they threw Jonah into the sea. And the wind stopped.

Then a great fish, sent by the Lord, swallowed Jonah. He was three days and three nights inside the fish. There Jonah prayed, "When my soul fainted, I remembered the Lord. Now I will offer my sacrifice. I will pay what I owe to the Lord.

For God is my deliverer." At last, the fish threw Jonah out upon the shore.

God again ordered Jonah to go to Nineveh. This time he obeyed. He went through the streets of the city, crying, "Yet forty days, and Nineveh shall be destroyed."

When the king and the people heard this, they were in great fear. The king ordered everyone in the city to do penance for his sins. Even the king did penance that God might forgive Nineveh. God saw that the people were sincere, and in His mercy He spared the city.

Jonah feared that he might be looked upon as a false prophet. He built a hut outside the city and waited there to see what would happen.

God caused an ivy to grow and shelter Jonah from the hot sun. For this Jonah was grateful. The next morning, God caused the ivy to wither. The sun beat down with such heat on Jonah that he cried, "It is better for me to die than to live."

God then said to him, "You are sorry for the ivy, although you were not the one to make it grow. Shall I not, therefore, spare Nineveh, which has more than one hundred twenty thousand people?"

Jonah, cast into the sea to save the sailors, was like Jesus Christ, who was sacrificed to redeem the world. Jonah was three days inside the fish; Christ was three days in the tomb.

The story of Jonah shows God's interest not only in Israel but in all mankind. It teaches that men must do penance for their sins. It also tells how God made use of His prophets, even when they did not want to carry out His messages.

An angel touches Isaiah's lips with a live coal, saying,
"Your sins shall be taken away."

38. ISAIAH AND JEREMIAH

GOD sent many prophets to the kingdoms of Israel and Judah. One of the greatest of these was a nobleman from Jerusalem. His name was Isaiah. He served as a prophet of God while four kings ruled over Judah.

One day Isaiah had a beautiful vision. He saw a high throne upon which the Lord was sitting. The robes of the Lord filled the Temple. Angels stood about the throne and sang, "Holy, holy, holy, Lord God of hosts, all the earth is full of His glory!"

The Temple shook with the sound of their voices and was filled with a bright cloud. Isaiah was afraid. He did not feel worthy to see such a vision. But one of the angels took a live coal from the altar. With it he touched the lips of Isaiah and said, "Your sins shall be taken away."

Besides bringing God's messages to the kings, Isaiah also preached to the people. He foretold that, like the kingdom of Israel, Judah also would be destroyed, but that a few people would be saved. Out of this small number God would make a new people who would serve Him faithfully. Isaiah spoke more about the Messiah and His kingdom than any other prophet.

After serving as God's prophet for many years, Isaiah was put to death by the wicked king, Manasseh.

Jeremiah was another of the great prophets. An angel touched his mouth and said, "Behold, I have put my words in your mouth." At the same time Jeremiah had a vision. He saw the message he was to carry to the nations. The prophet showed the people how ungrateful they had been to God. He told them that God was inviting them to come back to Him. Through Jeremiah, God made it known that He would destroy the country and send the people into captivity, but that God would restore to Jerusalem a few of His Chosen People. He would make them into a great nation which would have as its leader the Messiah Himself. Many times Jeremiah had to suffer because his message from God did not please the leaders. In his suffering Jeremiah was like our Lord.

Tobit instructs his son.

39. TOBIAH AND THE ANGEL

AMONG the captives who were carried off to Assyria there was a very saintly man named Tobit. He consoled his fellow captives and was very kind to them.

God allowed Tobit to become blind. When Tobit was already old, fearing that he would soon die, he called his son Tobiah and said, "Honor your mother always. Fear God and never sin. Give alms to the poor. Keep yourself from all impurity. Never let pride rule you. Do not do to another what you would not like him to do to you. Seek the advice of the wise man. Pray to God at all times, and ask Him to direct your ways. We are poor, but we shall possess much if we fear God and hate sin."

One day Tobit sent his son into a distant country to collect a debt. Since the young Tobiah did not know the way, God sent him the Angel Raphael to be his guide. On the journey

Raphael tells Tobiah to make a medicine with the fish.

they stopped at the river Tigris to rest and bathe. A large fish plunged after Tobiah, and he was frightened. But the angel told Tobiah to seize the fish. When he had drawn the fish on to the bank, the angel told him to take out its heart, gall, and liver to make a medicine.

They then continued the journey and arrived at the home of a relative of Tobiah. Tobiah took his daughter as his wife because the angel told him to do so.

Tobiah then returned home with his new wife. The angel told him to apply the medicine made from the fish to the eyes of his old father. At once his father's sight was restored.

Then the angel made himself known, saying, "I am the Angel Raphael, one of the seven who stand before the Lord." Raphael told the family how God had sent him to heal Tobit as a reward for his prayers and good works, and to guide the young Tobiah on his dangerous journey.

Judith shows the head of Holofernes to the people and urges them to praise God their Savior.

40. THE BRAVERY OF JUDITH

AN ASSYRIAN general, Holofernes, marched against Palestine. He laid siege to the city of Bethulia. The people of the city were in despair and decided to surrender if no help came within five days.

But there lived in that city a young and pious widow named Judith. When she heard that the city would be given up, she called together the leaders. She warned them that they were committing a great sin by not trusting in God. She urged them to do penance for this sin.

"Let us be patient and humble," she said, "and ask the Lord to show us mercy according to His will."

The leaders begged her, "Pray for us, for you are a holy woman."

Judith went home, put ashes on her head as a sign of penance, and prayed God for help. She asked God to make her strong and brave that she might save her people. Then she dressed herself in her finest clothes. With one of her maids she went to the enemy camp of the Assyrians and asked to be led to the general.

When Holofernes saw her, he was attracted by her beauty. He commanded that she be allowed to go and come as she wished.

Each night Judith prayed that God would guide her in this dangerous work. On the fourth night the general made a supper for his friends. He invited Judith also. After the feast the general, overcome with wine, fell into a deep sleep.

Judith waited till everybody had left. She stood weeping and praying, "Strengthen me, O Lord, that I may act according to Your will."

Then taking down the sword of Holofernes, she cut off his head. She went out and gave it to her maid to carry in a bag. They left the camp and went back to Bethulia.

All ran in great joy to meet Judith, for no one had expected her to return. She said, showing them the head of Holofernes, "Praise God, who has not forsaken them that hope in Him. Glorify Him, for His mercy lasts forever."

In the morning the people hung the head of Holofernes upon the city walls. All took up arms and went against the Assyrian camp. When the Assyrians found the headless body of their general, they were filled with terror and fled. In this way Judith saved her people.

The story of Judith is more than that of a brave woman. When the people of Bethulia depended only on their city walls and armed men, they were unable to protect the city. Judith with only trust in the help of God was able to defeat the strong army of the Assyrians.

When Holy Mother Church praises the Blessed Virgin Mary, she uses the very same words sung by the Israelites when Judith returned, "You are the glory of Jerusalem, you are the joy of Israel, you are the honor and glory of our people."

Suddenly there appear fingers writing upon the wall of the king's palace, like the hand of a man.

41. BELSHAZZAR'S BANQUET

ONE of the enemies of the Israelites was Nebuchadnezzar. He came from Babylon with his army and captured the city of Jerusalem. He carried away as captives many of the princes and nobles of Judah, including the Prophet Daniel.

Belshazzar succeeded Nebuchadnezzar as king and made a great feast for a thousand of his nobles. They all drank from the golden and silver vessels which were stolen from the temple in Jerusalem. They praised their gods of gold and silver and iron and stone.

Suddenly there appeared fingers, like the hand of a man, writing upon the wall of the king's palace. The king was afraid. He brought in the wise men of Babylon and said: "Whoever shall read this writing and let me know the meaning of it shall be honored in my kingdom." But none of them could explain the writing.

Then the queen told the king about Daniel, whom Belshazzar's father had made the prince of the wise men. Daniel was brought in before the king.

Daniel said, "O Belshazzar, you have turned against the Lord of heaven. The vessels of his house have been used for the drinking of wine, and false gods have been honored in this hall."

Then Daniel told the king the meaning of the words. "This is the writing that is written: MENE, TEKEL, PERES. Mene means that your kingdom is coming to an end. Tekel means that God has judged you and He was not pleased with you. Peres means that your kingdom is divided, and is given to the Medes and Persians."

Then the king gave great power to Daniel. But the same night Belshazzar was killed and his kingdom came to an end.

For six days Daniel remains in the lions' den unharmed.

42. DANIEL IN THE LIONS' DEN

DARIUS the Mede became king. He was pleased with Daniel and planned to make him governor-in-chief of a hundred and twenty princes. These princes tried to find some fault in Daniel that would make the king turn against him. But they could find nothing.

"We shall never find evidence against this Daniel," they said, "unless it is something in regard to the law of his God."

So they invented a decree that anyone who asked a favor of any god or man except Darius should be thrown into a den of lions. The king signed the decree, a law of the Medes and Persians, which could not be changed.

When Daniel heard of the decree, he went into his house, into his room where the windows were open toward Jerusalem, and knelt down in prayer as he always did three times a day. And there the princes saw him kneeling in prayer to God.

Then they went to the king and said, "This Daniel, one of your captives, does not respect you or your laws, but keeps on praying to his own God three times a day."

The king was worried and tried all day long to free him. But the princes gave him no peace. At last the king gave orders to throw Daniel into the den of lions. But to Daniel he said, "Your God, whom you serve faithfully, will save you!"

Then they put Daniel into the lions' den and brought a stone and put it at the entrance. The king sealed it with his own seal, so that Daniel could not escape.

For six days Daniel stayed in the lions' den, and the lions did not hurt him. But Daniel was hungry.

Far from Babylon, there lived a prophet named Habakkuk. He was taking some food to the workers in a field when an angel took him and put him in the den where Daniel was. He gave the food he carried to Daniel. Then the angel carried Habakkuk back to his house.

The unhappy king spent the night without sleep. Very early in the morning, on the seventh day, he hurried to the lions' den and called, "Daniel, O Daniel, servant of the living God, is your God whom you serve faithfully able to deliver you from the lions?"

"O king, live forever!" said Daniel. "The lions have not hurt me, because I was innocent in the sight of God and of my king!"

Now King Darius was very happy. He had Daniel brought out of the den and gave this command, "Let everyone in my kingdom worship the God of Daniel, for He is the living God! His kingdom shall have no end."

Daniel's enemies were thrown into the den, and the lions killed them at once.

43. THE RETURN TO JERUSALEM

THE Jews were in captivity for about seventy years. When Cyrus was king of Babylon, he allowed the Jews to return to their own country.

At the court of the Persian king lived a Jew, named Nehemiah. The king gave him permission to rebuild the city of Jerusalem, which had become a mass of ruins after its capture and destruction by the enemies of the Jews. He built a wall around Jerusalem.

Then the Jews started to rebuild the Temple on the same place where Solomon's Temple had stood. After twenty years, the new Temple was finished. The people dedicated the Temple with great joy and with many sacrifices.

From this time to the coming of Christ, the Jews were at different times ruled by Persia, Greece, Egypt, Syria, and Rome.

These were very sad years for the Jews. Their only comfort was the knowledge that the Messiah was soon to come. The prophets had told them so. Isaiah spoke more about the Messiah than any other prophet. He told them that the Messiah would be born of a virgin, and that He would be called Emmanuel, meaning God-with-us. He said that the Messiah would be a king, the prince of His people, the cornerstone on which the Church was to be built. He especially told how all other peoples besides the Chosen People would be invited to the kingdom of the Messiah, and how happy this kingdom would be.

Above all, Isaiah spoke of how the Messiah would die as a sacrifice for the sins of the world. His Kingdom would spread through the whole world and last till the end of time. This was the time when our Lord Jesus Christ was to come to teach, to bless, and to save mankind.

The New Testament

IN THE **Old Testament** you saw how God, in His goodness, promised to send a Redeemer to save mankind from sin, and how God prepared the way for Him. God entrusted the promise of a Redeemer to great men who were His faithful servants.

In the **New Testament** you will see how God kept His promise, how He sent into the world a Redeemer to save us from sin and make us God's children. This Redeemer is the greatest of all the kings, priests, and prophets whom God sent to guide men. He was not only a man; He was the Son of God who became man.

The life of Jesus, as it is written in the four Gospels by Saints Matthew, Mark, Luke, and John, tells you how our Redeemer, Jesus, was born, lived, and died for us, and how He rose from the dead. It tells you also of the doctrine He taught and of the Church, the Kingdom He founded.

The Angel Gabriel says to Mary, "Hail, full of grace!
The Lord is with you."

1. THE ANNUNCIATION

THE hour was at hand for which God had been preparing His people. Not only the Jews, but all the world was looking for a Redeemer. They prayed that God would now keep the promise He made to Adam and Eve and had repeated again and again through the prophets.

The Angel Gabriel was sent from God to the town of Nazareth, in that part of the land called Galilee, in the north. There the angel found a young girl named Mary, who was soon to be married to Joseph, a very good man who also lived in Nazareth. Though Joseph was a carpenter, he was a relative of King David. The angel came into the room where Mary was and said to her, "Hail, full of grace! The Lord is with you. You are blessed among women."

Mary was surprised at the angel's words and wondered what they could mean. Then the angel spoke again and said, "Do not be afraid, Mary. You have found grace with God. The Lord has chosen you to be the mother of a Son and you shall call Him Jesus. He shall be great; and shall be called the Son of God. The Lord will give Him the throne of David His father. He shall be king over the people of God forever; and of His kingdom there shall be no end."

But Mary could not see how all this would happen. And the angel said to her, "The Holy Spirit shall come upon you, and the power of the Most High God shall be over you; and the Holy One to be born shall be called the Son of God. And your cousin Elizabeth will also have a son in her old age, for nothing is impossible with God."

Mary was obedient. She knew that the angel was sent by God to tell her what God wanted. So she replied, "Behold the handmaid of the Lord. Be it done to me according to your word." And the angel departed from her.

As soon as Mary gave this answer, she became the Mother of God. The Second Person of the Blessed Trinity took to Himself a body and soul like ours. He became Man and dwelt among us. This is called the mystery of the Incarnation.

The coming of the angel to Mary is called the Annunciation, because the angel announced the birth of Jesus. The Church celebrates the feast of the Annunciation on March 25.

Mary visits Elizabeth who greets her with joy.

2. THE VISITATION

WHEN the angel had gone away, Mary at once made a four-day journey to the home of her cousin Elizabeth, eighty miles away in the south country. When Elizabeth saw Mary, she was filled with the Holy Spirit who let her know about the wonderful thing God had done to Mary. She cried out with joy, "Blessed are you among women, and blessed is the fruit of your womb! And how have I deserved to have the Mother of my Lord visit me?"

Then Mary was filled with the Holy Spirit and began to praise God, saying, "My soul praises the Lord and I rejoice in God, my Savior. Because He has looked upon the lowliness of His handmaid. For behold, from now on all generations shall call me blessed; because He who is mighty has done great things for me!"

Mary stayed with her cousin for nearly three months, until the birth of Elizabeth's son.

Nine months before an angel from God had appeared to Zechariah and told him that his wife, Elizabeth, would have a son who was to be called John. He was to convert many people and prepare them for the coming of the Savior. But Zechariah doubted these words, and from that moment he could not speak or hear. So now the relatives and friends asked him, by signs, what name he wished to be given to the child. He motioned for something to write upon; and when they brought it, he wrote, "John is his name."

Then all at once Zechariah could speak and hear again. He praised God, saying, "You, O child, shall be called a prophet of the Most High, to go before the Lord and to make ready His ways."

When John grew up, he went out into the desert to the south, and there he stayed until the time came for him to preach to the people, for this child became the great prophet, John the Baptist.

With Joseph, Mary adores her new-born Son Jesus.

3. THE BIRTH OF JESUS

SOON after the birth of John the Baptist, Joseph had a dream. He saw an angel from the Lord standing beside him. The angel said, "Joseph, son of David, do not be afraid to take Mary as your wife, for that which is begotten in her is of the Holy Spirit. And she shall bring forth a Son, and you shall call His name Jesus; for He shall save His people from their sins."

Joseph now knew that this Child who was to be born would be the King of Israel, of whom the prophets of the Old Testament had spoken so many times.

Soon after Joseph and Mary were married in Nazareth, a command went forth from the Emperor, Caesar Augustus, through all the lands of the Roman Empire. All the people were to go to the cities and towns from which their families had come, and there to have their names written down upon a list. Since both Joseph and Mary had come from the family of King David, they went together from Nazareth to Bethlehem. It was a long journey.

When Joseph and Mary came to Bethlehem, they found the city full of people who, like themselves, had come to have their names written upon the list. The inn was full, and there was no room for them. The best they could do was to go to a stable, where the cattle were kept. In this stable of Bethlehem Jesus, the Savior of the world, was born. Mary wrapped her Child in swaddling clothes and laid Him in a manger, where the cows and oxen were fed. Then she and Joseph adored the Divine Infant. This was the very first Christmas.

In this way the Son of God became Man. He came down to earth and was born of the Virgin Mary. Only lowly animals helped to warm the chill of the cave. For love of us, Jesus, true God, wanted to be born in a humble place. In this way He shows us how He loves humility.

Christmas is celebrated in memory of the birth of our Lord.

The shepherds find Mary and Joseph, and the little Babe.

4. THE SHEPHERDS

O N THAT night some shepherds were tending their sheep in a field near Bethlehem. Suddenly a great light shone upon them, and they saw an angel of the Lord standing before them. They were filled with fear, as they saw how glorious the angel was.

"Do not be afraid," said the angel, "for I am bringing you good news of great joy for all mankind. Today in the city of David is born a Savior, who is Christ the Lord. You will find an infant wrapped in swaddling clothes and lying in a manger."

And then they saw that the air around and the sky above them were filled with angels, praising God and singing: "Glory to God in the highest, and peace on earth among men of good will."

While they looked with wonder and listened, the angels went out of sight as suddenly as they had come. Then the shepherds said one to another, "Let us go over to Bethlehem and see this wonderful thing that God has made known to us."

As quickly as they could, they went to Bethlehem, and there they found Mary and Joseph, and the little Babe lying in the manger. They told Mary and Joseph, and others also, how they had seen the angels, and what they had heard about this Infant. All who heard their story wondered at it; but Mary, the Mother of the Child, said nothing. She thought over all these things and silently kept them in her heart. After their visit, the shepherds, praising God for the good news that He had sent to them, went back to their flocks.

In this way the birth of the Savior was made known to the faithful people who were praying for His coming. The Savior did not appear to the rich or powerful, but to plain, simple, and unknown shepherds. He was poor, and therefore He chose poor men as His friends. The poor and the humble are to be first in His kingdom.

The shepherds had great faith and devotion. In the childhood of Jesus they adored the great God of eternity; in His littleness they honored His humility; in His swaddling clothes they saw His poverty; in the hardness of the manger they wondered at His love of sacrifice. They drew close to Him and offered their little gifts with loving and grateful hearts.

Eight days passed. Then, according to the Law, Mary and Joseph held the religious service in which a Jewish child was given its name. They called the Child Jesus. The name Jesus means "Savior." It was the name the angel said He should have. The very name of this Child told what He would do for men. God had become Man to save the world.

Mary and Joseph bring Jesus to the temple to offer Him to the Lord.

5. THE PRESENTATION OF JESUS IN THE TEMPLE

IT WAS the law among the Jews that after the first child was born in a family, he should be brought to the Temple. God once told the Israelites that the first-born belonged to Him. The parents would offer a sacrifice to God as a sign that they were buying the child back. A rich man would offer a lamb, but a poor man might give a pair of young pigeons for the sacrifice. When Jesus was forty days old, Mary and Joseph brought Him to the Temple; and as Joseph the carpenter was not a rich man, they gave for the Child as an offering a pair of young pigeons.

At that time there lived in Jerusalem a man of God named Simeon. The Lord had spoken to him and had said to him that he would not die until the Anointed King had come. The word Christ means "Anointed." On a certain day the Spirit of the Lord told Simeon to go to the Temple. There he saw for the first time the promised Christ. He took the little Child Jesus in his arms and thanked God for letting him see the Redeemer. Then he said, "Now, O Lord, You may let Your servant die in peace, for my eyes have seen Your salvation, which You have sent to all people—a light to give light to all nations, the glory of Your people Israel."

When Mary and Joseph heard this, they wondered. Simeon gave them a blessing in the name of the Lord, and he said to Mary, "This little one shall cause many in Israel to fall and rise again. Many shall speak against Him; and sorrow shall pierce your heart like a sword."

All this was to happen later when Mary would see her Son dying on the cross.

A very old woman whose name was Anna, and to whom God spoke as to a prophet, also saw, through the help of the Holy Spirit, that this little Child was Christ the Lord, and she gave thanks to God for this grace.

So, early in the life of Jesus, God showed to a few that this little Child would become the Savior of His people and of the world.

The Magi offer Jesus gold, frankincense and myrrh.

6. WISE MEN FROM THE EAST

IN A country east of Judea, many miles away, there lived learned men who studied the stars. They were called Magi. One night they saw a strange star shining in the sky; and in some way they learned that the coming of the star meant that a King was soon to be born in Judea. They made the long journey with servants and camels and horses.

When the Magi reached Jerusalem, they asked the people, "Where is the newly born king of the Jews? For we have seen His star in the East and have come to worship Him."

But no one had heard of this new King. The news of their coming was sent to Herod, the King of Judea, who was now an old man. Herod was very wicked; and when he heard of someone born to be a king, he feared that he might lose his own kingdom. He made up his mind to kill this new King. He sent for the chief priests and scribes. After studying the books of the prophets, they said, "He is to be born in Bethlehem of Judea."

Then Herod sent for the wise men and said to them, "Go to Bethlehem, and there search carefully for the little Child; and when you have found Him, let me know, so that I also may come to worship Him."

The Magi went on their way toward Bethlehem, and suddenly they saw the star again shining upon the road before them. They were very happy and followed the star until it led them to the very house where the little Child was. They entered, and there they saw the little One, with Mary His Mother. They knew at once that this was the King, and they fell down on their faces and worshiped Him as the Lord. Then they brought out gifts of gold and precious perfumes, frankincense and myrrh, which were used in offering sacrifices, and they gave them as presents to the royal Child.

God sent a dream to the Magi, in which He told them not to go back to Herod, but to return home by another way. They obeyed the Lord and did not go back to the city.

Joseph arises, and takes the child and His Mother
by night, and withdraws into Egypt.

7. THE FLIGHT INTO EGYPT

SOON after the wise men had gone away, God sent another dream to Joseph. He saw an angel, who spoke to him, saying, "Rise up quickly; take the Child and His Mother, and go down to the land of Egypt, for Herod will try to find the little Child to kill Him."

At once Joseph rose up in the night, and took his wife and her Child, and quickly went with them down to Egypt. There they stayed as long as the wicked King Herod lived, which was not many months.

King Herod waited for the wise men to come back to him from their visit to Bethlehem, but he soon found that they had already gone to their home. This made Herod very angry. He sent out his soldiers to Bethlehem and commanded them to kill all the little children in Bethlehem who were two years old or younger, just to be sure that he would kill Jesus. What a cry went up to God from the mothers of these children who were torn from their arms and killed! These first martyrs who gave their lives for Jesus are called the Holy Innocents.

So when the soldiers came to the village and cruelly killed all the little children there, they did not kill the Child Jesus. He was far away by that time, lying safe and warm in His Mother's arms, journeying on to the distant country where King Herod's cruel hate could not reach Him.

Soon after King Herod died. The angel came again and spoke to Joseph in a dream, saying, "You may now take the Child back to His own land, for the king who wanted to kill Him is dead."

Then Joseph took his wife and the little Child Jesus, and began his journey back to the land of Judea. He was afraid to go to Bethlehem because the son of Herod was now ruling there. Instead he took his wife and the Child Jesus to Nazareth, which had been his own home town and that of Mary his wife, before the Child was born.

Jesus amazes the teachers of the law by His understanding and questions.

8. JESUS IS FOUND IN THE TEMPLE

WHEN Jesus was a boy, twelve years old, He was taken up to the feast of the Passover. For the first time He saw the holy city of Jerusalem and the Temple of the Lord. He knew He was in His Father's house.

The boy Jesus was so filled with love for His Father and the worship of the Temple that when it was time to go home to Nazareth, He stayed behind. The group of people who were traveling together was large, and at first He was not missed. But when night came and Jesus could not be found, His Mother became very much worried. The next day Mary and Joseph left their group and hurried back to Jerusalem. They sought Him among their friends and relatives who were living in the city, but could not find Him.

On the third day, still looking for their boy, they went up to the Temple. There they found Him, sitting with the teachers of the law, listening to their words and asking them questions. Everyone was surprised at this boy's knowledge of the word of God.

His Mother spoke to Him sadly, "Son, why have You treated us in this way? Your father and I have been seeking for You with sad hearts."

"Why did you look for Me?" said Jesus. "Did you not know that I must be about My Father's business?"

Jesus answered His Mother very gently. He thought she would have known that He must think about God's work, and surely she should have looked for Him first of all in His Father's house, for He was God's own Son. Yes, He was Mary's Son but He was God's Son, too. But when He had gently reminded her of this, He obediently went home to Nazareth with her.

Mary and Joseph did not understand these words, but Mary often thought about them afterward, for she treasured in her heart every word Jesus had spoken.

Jesus and His foster-father, Joseph, work in their carpenter shop.

9. THE HIDDEN LIFE OF JESUS

ALL that the Gospel tells us of the hidden life of Jesus at Nazareth is that "He was subject" to Mary and Joseph and that "He advanced in wisdom and age and grace before God and men." Jesus obeyed Mary and Joseph in all things. He helped His Mother in the home and learned the trade of a carpenter from Joseph.

God chose Joseph to be the foster-father of His Son, the husband of Mary, and the head of the Holy Family because he was "a just man." Joseph believed that the Child in his charge was the all-powerful Son of God and that Mary was the Mother of God. He worked diligently in his carpenter shop and did not expect a miracle to provide for Jesus and Mary. God chose a carpenter for the highest work on earth to show how much He respected labor.

In this quiet home Mary was always thinking about the things of God. She spent much of her time in prayer and in the work of the household. She left her home only for the works of piety, charity, and duty. Mary always showed the greatest love to Jesus and Joseph.

When Joseph died, Jesus, who was still a young man, took up the care of His Mother. In the work of the carpenter shop and the quiet life of a country village and the worship of the synagogue-church, He passed the years of His youth in humble obedience and labor.

The Holy Family of Nazareth is the model for all Christian families. They found their happiness in loving and serving God faithfully. In Jesus, Mary and Joseph, all mothers, fathers and children learn how to live a holy and happy family life, the center and soul of which is God.

The time finally came when Jesus was grown into a man and had to leave the quiet home of Nazareth and begin His Father's work. Out of a life of thirty-three years, He, who was Eternal Wisdom, chose to pass thirty years in silence, obedience, prayer, and labor. He was truly a hidden God!

John the Baptist baptizes Jesus in the river Jordan.

10. THE BAPTISM OF JESUS

THE news went through the land of Israel that a prophet had risen up and was preaching the word of God. For more than four hundred years God had not sent a prophet to His people. The new prophet was John, the son of the old priest Zechariah. From all parts of the land people came to the wild region beside the river Jordan, where John was preaching the word of God and the coming of the Messiah.

John was baptizing in the river Jordan. He poured water over the heads of those who were sorry for their sins. This was a sign of their hope to be cleansed of all sins. Because of this he was called "John the Baptist." John did not confer the Sacrament of Baptism, for our Lord had not yet instituted it.

Many who heard John believed him to be a great prophet, and others thought he was the promised Redeemer.

But John said, "I baptize you with water. But One greater than I is coming. He will baptize you with the Holy Spirit, and with fire." In these words he spoke of Jesus Christ.

One day Jesus Himself came to John. At once John knew that He was the Son of God. He refused to pour water over Him. He said to Jesus, "It is I who ought to be baptized by You, and do You come to me?"

But Jesus answered, "Let it be so now, for it is fitting that I should do all things that are right."

Then John baptized Jesus in the Jordan, as he had baptized others. And as Jesus came up out of the water and was praying, John saw above the head of Jesus the heavens opening and the Holy Spirit coming down like a dove and resting upon Him. And John heard a voice from heaven, saying, "This is My beloved Son, in whom I am well pleased."

And then John knew and told others that this was the Son of God, the Christ whom God had promised to send to the people.

Jesus says, "Begone Satan! It is written, 'The Lord your God shall you worship and Him alone shall you serve.'"

11. THE TEMPTATION OF JESUS IN THE DESERT

AFTER Jesus was baptized, the Holy Spirit led Him into the desert near the Jordan. There He was alone with God and planned out His work for the salvation of men. For forty days He ate nothing, so earnest was His union with God in prayer. But when the forty days were ended, suddenly He felt hungry.

At that moment Satan, the evil spirit, came to Jesus to tempt Him. "If You are the Son of God," said he, "command that these stones become loaves of bread."

Jesus answered, "Not by bread alone does man live, but by every word that comes forth from the mouth of God."

Jesus knew that power had been given to Him, to be used according to the Will of God.

Then the evil spirit led Jesus in thought to Jerusalem, the holy city, and brought Him to the top of a high tower on the Temple and said to Him, "Now show all the people that You are the Son of God by throwing Yourself down to the ground. You know that it is written in the book of Psalms, 'He shall give His angels charge over You; and upon their hands they shall bear You up, lest You dash Your foot against a stone.'"

Jesus answered, "It is written further, 'You shall not tempt the Lord your God.'"

The evil spirit led Him to the top of a high mountain and caused a vision of all the kingdoms of the world and their glory to stand before the eyes of Jesus. Then he said, "All these things will I give You, if You fall down and worship me."

But Jesus said to him, "Begone, Satan! It is written, 'The Lord your God shall you worship and Him alone shall you serve.'"

When Satan found that Jesus would not listen to him, he left Him. Then the angels of God came to Jesus in the desert and gave Him the food that He needed.

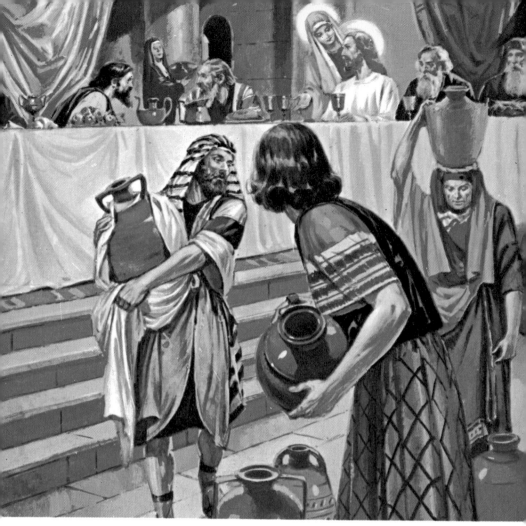

Mary says to Jesus, "They have no wine."

12. THE MARRIAGE AT CANA

A FEW days after Jesus met His first disciples at the river Jordan, He went with them to a town in Galilee called Cana, to be present at a wedding.

The Mother of Jesus was at this wedding as a friend of the family, for Nazareth, where she lived, was near Cana. Before the wedding feast was over, all the wine had been used. Mary understood how badly these people felt. The Mother of Jesus believed that her Son had power to do whatever He wished, and she said to Him, "They have no wine."

Jesus said to her, "What would you have Me do? My hour has not yet come."

It was not yet time for so public a miracle. However, at the request of His Mother, Jesus was willing to help.

But since His Mother knew that Jesus would in some way help the people in their need, she said to the servants who were waiting at the table, "Do whatever He tells you."

In the dining hall were standing six large stone jars, each about as large as a barrel, holding twenty-five gallons. These jars held water for washing. Jesus said to the servants, "Fill the jars with water."

The servants obeyed Jesus and filled the jars up to the brim. Then Jesus spoke to them again and said, "Now pour out what you need from the jars and take it to the chief steward of the feast."

They drew out from the jars some of the water, which they had poured into them, and saw that it had been turned into wine. As the chief steward did not know where the servants got the wine, he said to the young man who had just been married, "At a feast everybody gives his best wine first, and later he brings on wine that is not so good; but you have kept the good wine until now."

This was the first time that Jesus used the power that God had given Him, to do what no other man could do. Such works as these are called "miracles," and Jesus did them as signs of His power as the Son of God. When the disciples saw this miracle, they believed in Jesus more fully than before.

Jesus changed water into wine at His Mother's request, to teach us how much He loves her and how powerful are her prayers.

Jesus drives the buyers and sellers out of the Temple.

13. THE SELLERS IN THE TEMPLE

JESUS and His disciples went up to Jerusalem to attend the feast of the Passover. There, in the courts of the Temple, Jesus found men who were selling oxen and sheep and doves for the sacrifices. Other men were sitting at tables, changing the money of the Jews who came from other lands into the money of Judea. All this made the courts around the Temple seem like a market and not a place for the worship of God.

Jesus picked up some cord and made from it a whip. With it He began to drive out of the Temple all the buyers and sellers. He drove out the sheep and the oxen. He overturned the tables and threw the money on the floor. To those who were selling the doves He said, "Take these things away, and do not make the House of My Father a house of business."

The rulers of the Jews were angry because many of them were getting rich by this selling of offerings and changing of money. Some of the rulers came to Jesus and said to Him, "What right have You to come here and do these things? What sign can You show that God has given You this power?"

Jesus said to them, "Destroy this Temple, and in three days I will raise it up."

Then the Jews said, "It has taken forty-six years to build this Temple, and will You raise it up in three days?"

But Jesus did not mean the Temple. He was speaking of Himself, for in Him God was dwelling as in a temple. He meant that when they put Him to death, He would rise again in three days.

The Pharisees and Scribes were jealous of Jesus because the people loved Him. He was everybody's Friend. They found fault with Him because He went with publicans and sinners, though they knew well He did so only to make them give up their sins and turn to God. The Pharisees came to hate Jesus so much that they planned to put Him to death.

Nicodemus comes to speak to Jesus by night.

14. NICODEMUS COMES TO JESUS

NICODEMUS, a ruler of the Jews and a Pharisee, went to Jesus one night and said, "Teacher, we know that God sent You, for no one could work the miracles that You do unless God were with him."

Jesus said to him, "Unless a man is born again from above, he cannot see the Kingdom of God."

"How can a man be born again?" Nicodemus asked.

Jesus replied, "Unless a man is born through water and the Spirit, he cannot enter the Kingdom of God." Then Jesus went on to explain: since God is above, the only way that one can enter His Kingdom is to be born from above. What is on the natural level, the level of flesh, cannot reach the divine level without being raised.

This lifting up is done by God coming down from heaven to man, and then returning again to heaven, drawing man up with Him. This is the Incarnation, that is, the Son of God becoming Man; the Redemption, that is, the God-Man offering His life to save the world from sin and death; the Resurrection and the Ascension, that is, Jesus raised to life and returning to His Father in glory.

This new birth must be brought about by water and the Holy Spirit. Water refers to the sacrament of Baptism. No one can be a child of God without a new heart. If we believe in Jesus, the Holy Spirit gives us a new heart. We become children of God through the grace of Baptism.

So Jesus went on to say, "The Son of Man must be lifted up as Moses lifted up the serpent in the desert, so that everyone who believes may have eternal life in Him. Yes, God loved the world so much that He gave His only Son, so that everyone who believes in Him may not be lost but may have eternal life."

Nicodemus did believe in Jesus. He was born again, and became a child of God.

Jesus tells the Samaritan woman about the living water that He will give to men.

15. THE SAMARITAN WOMAN

NE morning, Jesus stopped to rest beside an old well at the foot of a mountain. His disciples had gone to the village to buy food.

Just at this moment a Samaritan woman came to the well with her water jar upon her head. Jesus said to her, "Please give Me a drink."

She said to Him, "How is it that You, who are a Jew, ask drink of me, a Samaritan woman?"

Jesus answered, "If you only knew the gift of God, and who asks you for a drink, you would have asked of Him, and He would have given you living water."

The woman said, "Sir, You have nothing to draw with, and the well is deep. From where, then, do You have living water?"

"Whoever drinks of this water," said Jesus, "shall thirst again; but whoever drinks of the water that I shall give him, shall never thirst."

"Sir," said the woman, "give me some of this water that I may not thirst, or come here to draw."

Jesus told her the sins that she had committed. Much surprised, she said, "Sir, I see that You are a prophet. I know that when the Messiah comes, He will tell us all things."

Jesus said, "I who speak with you am He."

Just at this time the disciples of Jesus came back from the village. Jesus said to them, "My food is to do the will of Him who sent Me, to accomplish His work."

When the Samaritan woman went to the town, she said to the people, "Come and see a Man who has told me all that I have ever done. Can He be the Christ?"

Soon the woman came back to the well with many of her people. They asked Jesus to come to their town and to stay there and teach them. He went with them and stayed two days. Many of the people believed in Jesus and said, "We have heard for ourselves; now we know that this is indeed the Savior of the world."

It was in this way that Jesus first made Himself known as a messenger from God. Although the Jews had read in the Psalms that the Savior was to be God's Son, they had come to look for Him as an earthly king. They did not understand how God could live among them as a man. They also expected the Messiah to free them from the power of the Romans. Jesus wanted to teach them that He was really God and that His kingdom was not of this world. He waited until their faith was stronger before telling them His full message.

During this time the rulers of the Jews, and especially the Scribes and Pharisees, began to be His enemies. But Jesus was the great and kind Teacher — the Son of God, going among the people He came to save. He loved the sinners, the poor, and the suffering.

The disciples follow Jesus' suggestion and catch many fishes.

16. THE GREAT CATCH OF FISH

ONE day Jesus sat in a boat and talked to the people from it as they sat on the beach. After He had finished speaking, He said to Peter, "Row out into deep water, and lower your nets for a catch." Peter told Jesus that they had been out on the lake all night and had caught nothing. "But," he said, "if You say so, I will lower the nets."

They caught so many fish that the nets were breaking. They called James and John, the two brothers, who were in the other boat, to help them. They came and filled the two boats until they nearly sank.

When Peter saw this, he fell at the knees of Jesus saying, "Leave me, Lord. I am a sinful man." "Do not be afraid," said Jesus, "from now on you will be catching men." Jesus said to Peter and the others, "Follow Me." They left everything and became His followers.

One evening Jesus went alone to a mountain not far from Capernaum. A crowd of people and His disciples followed Him. But Jesus left them all and went up to the top of the mountain, where He could be alone. There He stayed all night, praying to God, His Father. In the morning, out of all His followers, He chose twelve men who were to walk with Him and listen to His words, so that they might be able to teach others. Some of these men He had called before; but now He called them again, and others with them. They were called "The twelve," or "the disciples." After Jesus went to heaven, they were called "The apostles," a word which means "those who were sent out," because Jesus sent them out to preach the Gospel to the world.

Jesus later sent seventy-two other disciples, two by two, into the cities and villages, to preach the kingdom of God.

One leper returns and thanks Jesus for making him well.

17. THE TEN LEPERS

AS JESUS was entering a certain village on His way to Jerusalem, ten lepers met him. They were not allowed to live among other people because of their disease, so they stood far away and cried out with a loud voice, "Jesus, master, have pity on us."

And when Jesus saw them He had pity on them and told them to come closer. He then said to them, "Go, show yourselves to the priests that they may declare that you are clean again and cured of your disease."

On their way they were cured. They were so happy that they did not even think of coming back to Jesus to thank Him. Only one of them, seeing that he was made clean, returned and bowed low before Jesus and thanked Him with all his heart. And he was not even a Jew, but a Samaritan.

Then Jesus asked, "Were not the ten made clean? But where are the nine? Did no one come back and thank God except this foreigner?"

And Jesus said to him, "Arise, go your way, for your faith has saved you."

At another time while Jesus was on His journey of preaching in Galilee, a leper came to Him, saying, "O Lord, if You are willing, I know that You can make me well and clean!"

Jesus was full of pity. He reached out His hand and touched him and said, "I am willing; be clean!" And in a moment all the scales of leprosy fell away, his skin became pure, and the leper stood up a well man. Jesus said to him, "Tell no one, but go to the priests, and offer the gift that the law commands, and let them see that you have been cured."

But this leper who had been healed could not keep still. He told everybody whom he knew that Jesus, the great prophet, had taken away his leprosy.

Jesus speaks to the cripple and heals him.

18. THE CRIPPLE AT THE POOL

WHILE Jesus was at Jerusalem, He saw in the city, not far from the Temple, a pool called Bethsaida. Beside this pool were five porches in which were lying a great crowd of sick and blind, helpless and crippled people. At certain times the water rose and bubbled up in the pool, at which time the spring had power to cure diseases. It was said that an angel came down to move the water and gave it the power to heal. The first to go down into the pool after the water was moved was cured.

On the Sabbath day Jesus walked among these poor, suffering people, who were waiting for the water to rise. Jesus looked at a man who had been a cripple for almost forty years, and said to him, "Do you wish to be made well?"

The man did not know who Jesus was. He answered, "Sir, I have no one to put me into the pool when the water is moved; for while I am trying to crawl down, someone steps before me."

Jesus said to the man, "Rise, take up your mat and walk!"

As these words were spoken, the cripple felt a new power in his limbs. He rose up, took the piece of matting on which he had been lying, rolled it up, and walked away toward his home.

The Jews said, "Who was this man who told you to carry your mat on the Sabbath day?"

The man who had been cured did not know who it was who cured him, for Jesus had walked away. Jesus met this man later and said to him, "You have been cured. Sin no more, or something worse will come upon you."

The man went away from the Temple and told the Jews that it was Jesus who had made him well. The Jews were very angry at Jesus because He had cured this man on the Sabbath. But Jesus said to them, "My Father works on all days to do good to men, and I work also."

Jesus preaches to His disciples and to a great crowd of people gathered on a mountain.

19. THE SERMON ON THE MOUNT

ON THE mountain Jesus preached to His disciples and to the great crowd of people who had gathered there. Jesus spoke of the kingdom of God and how men must live who become members of it.

"Blessed are the poor in spirit, for theirs is the kingdom of heaven.

"Blessed are the meek, for they shall possess the earth.

"Blessed are they who mourn, for they shall be comforted.

"Blessed are they who hunger and thirst for justice, for they shall be satisfied.

"Blessed are the merciful, for they shall obtain mercy.

"Blessed are the pure of heart, for they shall see God.

"Blessed are the peacemakers, for they shall be called children of God.

"Blessed are they who suffer persecution for justice' sake, for theirs is the kingdom of heaven.

"Blessed are you when men reproach you, and persecute you, and, speaking falsely, say all manner of evil against you, for My sake. Rejoice and exult, because your reward is great in heaven; for so did they persecute the prophets who were before you."

To His disciples Jesus said:

"You are the salt of the earth; but if the salt loses its strength, what shall it be salted with?

"You are the light of the world . . . Let your light shine before men, in order that they may see your good works and give glory to your Father in heaven."

To the people Jesus said:

"Do not be anxious, saying, 'What shall we eat?' or, 'What shall we drink?' or, 'What are we to put on?' for your Father knows that you need all these things. But seek first the kingdom of God and His justice, and all these things shall be given you besides."

Jesus astonishes the crowds by His teaching.

20. JESUS TEACHES CHARITY

JESUS continued His Sermon on the Mount with His teaching on the love of our neighbor. He said, "If you are offering your gift at the altar, and there you remember that your brother has anything against you, leave your gift before the altar and go first to be reconciled to your brother, and then come and offer your gift.

"You have heard that it was said, 'You shall love your neighbor, and hate your enemy.' But I say to you, love your enemies, do good to those who hate you, and pray for those who persecute you, so that you may be children of your Father in heaven, who makes His sun to rise on the good and the evil, and sends rain on the just and the unjust. For if you love those who love you, what reward shall you have? You, therefore, are to be perfect, even as your heavenly Father is perfect.

"If you forgive men their offenses, your heavenly Father will also forgive you your offenses. But if you do not forgive men, neither will your Father forgive you your offenses.

"Do not judge, that you may not be judged. For with what judgment you judge, you shall be judged.

"Therefore, all that you wish men to do to you, even so do you also to them; for this is the Law and the Prophets.

"Not everyone who says to Me, 'Lord, Lord,' shall enter the kingdom of heaven; but he who does the will of My Father in heaven shall enter the kingdom of heaven.

"Everyone, therefore, who hears these My words and acts upon them, shall be likened to a wise man who built his house on rock. And the rain fell, and the floods came, and the winds blew and beat against that house, but it did not fall, because it was founded on rock."

When Jesus had finished these words, the crowds were astonished at His teaching; for He was teaching them as one having authority and not as their Scribes and Pharisees.

The Roman centurion entreats Jesus to cure his servant from afar.

21. THE CENTURION'S SERVANT

THERE was at Capernaum an officer of the Roman army, a man who had under him a company of a hundred men. They called him a "centurion." He was not a Jew, but was what the Jews called a "Gentile," that is, a foreigner, a name which the Jews gave to all people outside of their own race.

This Roman centurion was a good man, and he loved the Jews because through them he had heard of God and how to worship Him. Out of his own money he built a synagogue for the Jews.

The centurion had a young servant, a boy, whom he loved very much. This boy was sick with a palsy and near death. The centurion had heard that Jesus could cure those who were sick; so he asked the chief men of the synagogue, who were called its "elders," to go to Jesus and ask Him to come and cure his servant.

The centurion himself also entreated Him, saying, "Lord, my servant is lying sick in the house, paralyzed, and is grievously afflicted."

Then Jesus said, "I will go and heal him."

But in answer the centurion said, "Lord, I am not worthy that You should come under my roof; but only say the word, and my servant will be healed. For I too am a man subject to authority, and have soldiers subject to me; and I say to one, 'Go,' and he goes; and to another, 'Come,' and he comes; and to my servant, 'Do this,' and he does it."

When Jesus heard this, He wondered at this man's faith. He turned to the people following Him and said, "I have not found such great faith in Israel."

Then Jesus said to the centurion, "Go your way; as you have believed, so be it done to you."

And the servant was healed in that very hour.

Jesus says to Matthew, "Follow Me."

22. THE CALL OF MATTHEW

A MAN named Matthew sat by the side of one of the main roads near Capernaum. Every day he collected taxes from the Jews for the Roman government. Jesus happened to walk along this road with His friends. He said to Matthew, "Follow Me."

Matthew got up and followed Jesus at once. Many years later he wrote the Gospel that appears first in the New Testament, telling about the life of Jesus.

The first thing that Matthew did after Jesus called him to be a disciple was to invite Jesus and the rest of the disciples to a fine dinner in honor of his new Master. Most of his guests were tax collectors or publicans like himself, and no people were more scorned than these publicans because they worked for the Roman government.

When the Pharisees saw Jesus eating with Matthew and his friends, they asked the disciples, "Why does your Master eat with tax collectors and sinners?"

Jesus did not wait for His disciples to answer. He said, "It is not the healthy who need the doctor, but the sick. Go and learn the meaning of the words: What I want is mercy, not sacrifice. I did not come to call the virtuous, but sinners."

Jesus came to this earth for the purpose of destroying sin, the work of the devil, and to bring grace and salvation through His Death and Resurrection, that we may live a holy life as children devoted to doing His Father's will.

The poor Lazarus begs for scraps from the rich man's table.

23. THE RICH MAN AND LAZARUS

JESUS told the Pharisees this parable to teach them that God knew their hearts even though they appeared to be holy in the eyes of people and were really not.

There was a rich man who used to dress in purple and fine linen and feasted every day. A beggar named Lazarus, covered with sores, lay at his gate. He longed to fill himself with the scraps that fell from the rich man's table. Dogs even came and licked his sores. Then the beggar died and angels carried him to the bosom of Abraham. The rich man also died and was buried.

From the abode of the dead where he was in torments, the rich man saw Abraham with Lazarus. So he cried out, "Father Abraham, pity me and send Lazarus to dip the tip of his finger in water and cool my tongue."

"My son," Abraham replied, "remember that you received your good things in your lifetime, but Lazarus received what was bad. Now he is being comforted here while you are in agony. Besides, there is no crossing from your side to ours."

The rich man replied, "Father, I beg you then to send Lazarus to my father's house, since I have five brothers, to warn them so that they may not come to this place of torment too."

"They have Moses and the Prophets," Abraham answered, "let them hear them."

"No, Father Abraham," replied the rich man, "but if someone goes to them from the dead, they will repent."

Then Abraham said to him, "If they will not listen either to Moses or to the Prophets, they will not be convinced even if someone should rise from the dead."

The penitent woman bathes the feet of Jesus and anoints them
with costly perfume.

24. THE PENITENT WOMAN

ONE day a Pharisee, named Simon, asked Jesus to come and to take dinner at his house. While Jesus was at the table, a woman came into the dining room. Kneeling at the feet of Jesus, she wept tears of sorrow for her many sins, and the tears fell upon His feet. She dried His feet with her hair, and kissed them. Afterwards she broke a beautiful jar of costly perfume and anointed His feet by pouring the perfume upon them.

Simon, the Pharisee, knew that this woman was a great sinner. He was surprised when he saw that Jesus allowed her to weep at His feet and to anoint them with perfume.

Jesus knew about Simon's thoughts, and said, "Simon, there was a certain rich man who had loaned one man a great sum of money, and another man only a small amount. Since neither of the two men could pay back the money, he freely forgave them both. Which of these two men loved the rich man more?"

"I suppose," answered Simon, "that the man to whom he forgave the bigger debt loved him more."

"You are right," said Jesus. Then He turned to the sinful woman still weeping at His feet, and said, "Simon, when I came into your home you did not treat Me like an honored guest. You did not give Me water to wash the dust from My feet; but this woman has washed My feet with her tears and has dried them with the hair of her head. You did not give Me a kiss of welcome; but this woman has kissed My feet. You did not anoint My head with oil, as you anoint the heads of your friends who come to visit you; but this woman has poured costly perfume upon My feet. Wherefore I say to you, her sins, many as they are, shall be forgiven her, because she has loved much. But he to whom little is forgiven, loves little."

And Jesus said to the woman, "Your sins are forgiven. Your faith has saved you; go in peace."

Jesus raises the widow's son from the dead.

25. THE WIDOW'S SON

JUST as Jesus and His disciples came near to the gate of the city of Naim, they were met by a crowd of people who were carrying out the body of a dead man to be buried. He was a young man, and the only son of his mother, and she was a widow.

When Jesus saw the mother in her grief, He pitied her and said, "Do not weep."

The bearers looked with wonder on this stranger and set down the stretcher. Standing beside the body, Jesus said, "Young man, I say to you, arise."

And in a moment the young man sat up and began to speak. Jesus gave him to his mother, who now saw that her son, who had been dead, was alive again.

A great fear came upon all who had looked upon this wonderful work of Jesus.

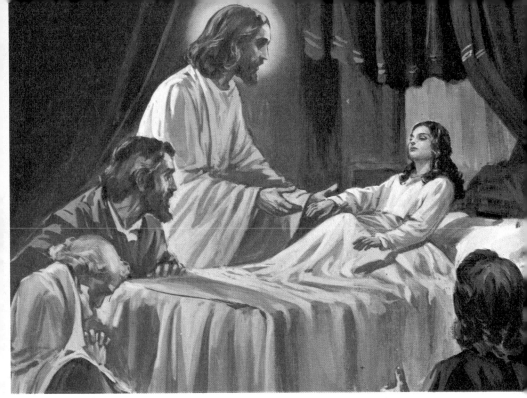

Jesus brings back to life the daughter of Jairus.

26. THE DAUGHTER OF JAIRUS

A MAN named Jairus fell down at the feet of Jesus and said, "Master, come to my house at once! My little daughter is dying; but if You will come and lay Your hands upon her, she will live."

While he was yet speaking, someone came to him and said, "Your daughter is dead."

But Jesus said to Jairus, "Do not be afraid; only believe, and she will yet be saved to you."

Jesus took with Him three of His disciples, Peter, James, and John, and the father and mother of the child. On the couch was lying the dead body of a girl, twelve years old. Our Lord took her by the hand and spoke to her, "Little girl, rise up!"

And life returned to the little girl. She opened her eyes and sat up.

Jesus tells the man to stretch out his hand.

27. THE MAN WITH A WITHERED HAND

ONE Sabbath day Jesus went to the synagogue as usual. As He stood up in the synagogue He could plainly see a man whose right hand was withered and useless. The man was hoping that Jesus would heal his hand.

The scribes and Pharisees were also there, watching Jesus. They had rules concerning what could and could not be done on the Sabbath. According to those rules, no cure could be worked. So they were hoping that Jesus would cure the man. Then they could accuse Him of breaking the rules of the Sabbath, of not being a good person.

Jesus knew what they were thinking. He said to them, "Is it against the law on the Sabbath to do good, or to do evil; to save life or to destroy it?"

He went on to point out that the scribes and Pharisees themselves allowed a man to pull his sheep out of a pit on the Sabbath. Yet how much more precious is a human being than a sheep! "Clearly," He concluded, "good deeds may be performed on the Sabbath."

No one was able to refute His reasoning. So Jesus turned to the man and said, "Stretch out your hand." The man lifted his helpless hand, which he had not been able to use for many years. It was perfectly cured.

The Pharisees were angry that their rules had been broken. They stormed out of the synagogue and met together with others who hated Jesus. Together they plotted how they could destroy Him.

But Jesus went down to the Sea of Galilee. As word of His miracles spread, His fame grew and great crowds followed Him. His enemies did not dare to kill Him.

The apostles beg Jesus for help, and He, standing up,
calms the storm.

28. JESUS CALMS THE STORM

WHEN the evening came, after teaching all day, Jesus saw that the crowds of people were still pressing around Him, and there was no time for Him to rest. Jesus said to His disciples, "Let us cross over to the other side of the lake, where we can be alone."

So they took Jesus into the boat and began to row across the Sea of Galilee. While they were rowing, Jesus fell asleep. It had been very calm when they started. But when they were half way across, a great wind blew down from between the high hills that were around the lake. The storm drove great waves of water into the boat, so that it was in danger of sinking, but Jesus slept on. The apostles were afraid. They felt sure they were going to be drowned. They awoke Jesus, saying, "Lord, save us! We are perishing!" They knew from His miracles that He could do something for them.

Jesus stood up and looked out upon the sea. He then said to the waves, "Peace, be still!"

At once the wind stopped blowing, the waves were quiet, and there was a great calm.

Jesus said to His disciples, "Why are you afraid? Why do you have so little faith in Me?"

The disciples were amazed and said to each other, "Who is this man whom even the winds and the sea obey?" They had seen men and even devils obey our Lord. This time even wind and sea obeyed His voice. Again the disciples could see who Jesus was. Only God can make the winds and the seas obey. Their faith was strengthened, and they worshipped our Lord. They needed this faith, for the enemies of Jesus were becoming more and more active against Him.

When our Lord and the apostles returned from the other side of the lake, a great crowd saw Jesus and gathered around Him. They brought to Him their sick, and He cured them.

Jesus comes to cure the possessed man.

29. A POSSESSED MAN

JESUS and His apostles sailed to the country of the Gerasenes, which is opposite Galilee. When they landed they met a man who for a long time had been possessed by a devil. He lived in tombs, not in a house, and he did not want to wear clothes. Many times the devil would take hold of the man so that he had to be bound with chains and kept under guard. But he would break the bonds, and would be driven by the devil into the desert.

When the possessed man saw Jesus, he fell down before Him, and cried out with a loud voice, "What have I to do with You, Jesus, Son of the Most High God? I beg you, do not torment me."

Jesus asked the man, "What is your name?"

"Legion," he said, because many devils had entered him. These devils begged Jesus not to command them to depart into the abyss.

A herd of many swine was feeding on the mountainside. The devils kept begging Jesus to let them enter into them. And Jesus gave them leave. At once the devils came out of the man and entered into the swine. The swine then rushed down the cliff into the lake and were drowned.

When the swineherds saw what had happened, they fled and reported it in the town and in the country. The people came out to see what had happened. When they came to Jesus, they found the man from whom the devils had gone out sitting at His feet, clothed and in his right mind; and they were frightened.

Those who had seen what had happened told them how the man had been saved from Legion. Then all the people of the Gerasene district begged Jesus to leave because they were afraid.

The head of John the Baptist is brought to the daughter of Herodias.

30. THE BEHEADING OF JOHN THE BAPTIST

JOHN the Baptist was put in prison by the king, Herod Antipas, because of Herodias, his brother Philip's wife, whom he had married. For John said to Herod, "It is not lawful for you to have your brother's wife." Herod feared John, knowing that he was a just and holy man. But Herodias wanted to put him to death.

John sent two of his followers to Jesus to ask Him if He was really the Savior who was to come. Jesus said to them, "Go and report to John what you have heard and seen: the blind see, the lame walk, the lepers are cleansed, the deaf hear, the dead rise, the poor have the Gospel preached to them. And blessed is he who is not scandalized in Me." As they went away, Jesus spoke about John: "This is he of whom it is written, 'Behold, I send My messenger before Your face, who shall make ready Your way before You.'"

John the Baptist was in prison nearly a year when a great feast was held on King Herod's birthday, and all the princes and nobles of his kingdom were in the palace, eating and drinking together. The young daughter of Herodias came into the supper room and danced before the guests. Herod was so much pleased with her dancing that he said to her, "Ask whatever you want, and I will give it to you, even though it be half of my kingdom."

Her mother told her what to ask, and she quickly came back to the king and said, "I want you at once to give me on a dish the head of John the Baptist."

The king was ashamed to break his word in the presence of his princes. He sent a man to the prison with orders that the head of John the Baptist should be cut off and brought. It was done; and the young girl took it upon a dish and gave it to her mother.

The followers of John went to the prison and took away his body and buried it. After this they were among the followers of Jesus.

Jesus feeds over five thousand people with only five loaves and two fishes.

31. THE MIRACLE OF THE LOAVES AND FISHES

WHEN Jesus saw how eager the crowds were to hear Him, taking pity on them, He taught them and healed the sick. Toward evening, some of the apostles asked Jesus to send the crowd away, for it was near their suppertime.

But Jesus said to them, "They need not go away. You can give them food to eat."

Philip looked at the great crowd, over five thousand men, besides women and children, and he said, "Thirty dollars' worth of bread would not be enough to give to everyone even a little piece."

Then another of the apostles, Andrew, Peter's brother, said to Jesus, "There is a boy here who has five loaves of barley bread and two dried fishes. But what use would they be among so many people?"

Jesus said to the apostles, "Go out among the people and divide them into groups of fifty and a hundred, and tell them to sit down."

So the people all sat down upon the green grass, and they watched Jesus as He took into His hands the five loaves and the two fishes which the boy had brought. He looked up to heaven to thank His Father and blessed the food. He then broke the loaves and the dried fishes and gave the pieces to the apostles. They went among the people and gave to everyone bread and fish, as much as each needed. So they all ate and had enough.

Then Jesus said, "Gather up the pieces of food that are left, so that nothing may be wasted."

Twelve baskets of food were left. The crowds rushed toward our Lord to take Him and force Him to be their king. But He hid Himself from the people.

Jesus walks on the water toward the apostles.

32. JESUS WALKS ON THE WATER

DURING a great storm the apostles were in a boat on the lake. They saw Jesus coming toward them, walking upon the water. Thinking it was a spirit, they were afraid. But Jesus called out, "Take courage; it is I, do not be afraid." Then they knew that it was their Master.

Peter cried out to Jesus, "Lord, if it be You, let me come over to You on the water." Jesus said to Peter, "Come."

Peter leaped overboard and he, too, walked on the water to go to Jesus. But when he saw the high waves, he became frightened. As he began to sink, he cried, "Lord, save me!"

Jesus reached out His hand and lifted him up, saying, "O man of little faith, why did you doubt My word?"

When Jesus came on board the boat with Peter, at once the wind ceased and the sea was calm. The apostles fell down before Him and said, "In truth You are the Son of God!"

Standing in a boat, Jesus instructs the people.

33. JESUS PREACHES FROM A BOAT

THE Pharisees were very angry because Jesus was working miracles and drawing the people to Himself. They had a meeting to find out how they could put Jesus to death.

Knowing this, Jesus with His disciples went to the seashore. And a large crowd followed Him from all parts of Palestine and even from other countries.

Jesus told His disciples to have a small boat ready for Him because of the great crowd that gathered around Him. He preached to them from the boat.

The people were pressing upon Jesus to touch Him. They brought to Him all the sick suffering from many diseases and He cured them.

Even those with an unclean spirit fell down before Him and cried out, "You are the Son of God!"

"I am the living bread that has come down from heaven. If anyone eat of this bread he shall live forever; and the bread that I will give is My flesh for the life of the world."

34. THE PROMISE OF THE HOLY EUCHARIST

JESUS came again to Capernaum and went into the synagogue, which was full of people, some of whom had eaten of the five loaves. These people wanted Jesus to feed them in the same way again, but He said to them, "You seek Me because you have eaten of the loaves. Do not labor for the food that perishes, but for that which endures unto life everlasting, which the Son of Man will give you."

They said to Him, "Lord, give us always this bread."

But He answered, "I am the living bread that has come down from heaven. If anyone eat of this bread he shall live forever; and the bread that I will give is My Flesh for the life of the world."

The Jews argued with one another, saying, "How can this man give us His Flesh to eat?"

Our Lord did not change the meaning of His words. Instead He said what He meant with even stronger words, "Amen, amen, I say to you, unless you eat the Flesh of the Son of Man, and drink His Blood, you shall not have life in you. He who eats My Flesh and drinks My Blood has life everlasting, and I will raise him up on the last day. For My Flesh is food indeed, and My Blood is drink indeed. He who eats My Flesh, and drinks My Blood, abides in Me and I in him."

When the people heard this, many of them said, "This is too hard to believe." And they began to depart.

Jesus then turned to His apostles and asked, "Do you also wish to go away?"

Peter answered, "Lord, to whom shall we go? You have words of everlasting life, and we have come to believe and to know that You are the Christ, the Son of God."

At this time Jesus promised the Most Holy Eucharist. This promise was later fulfilled at the Last Supper.

Peter says Jesus is the Son of the living God, and Jesus makes him the head of His Church.

35. PETER, THE HEAD OF THE CHURCH

ONE day, Jesus and His apostles arrived at a place called Caesarea Philippi. There Jesus asked His apostles this question, "Who do men say the Son of Man is?" This was the name by which Jesus often spoke of Himself.

They answered Him, "Some say John the Baptist; and others, Elijah; and others, Jeremiah, or one of the prophets."

Then He said to them, "But who do you say that I am?"

Simon Peter answered and said, "You are the Christ, the Son of the living God."

Jesus said to Peter, "Blessed are you, Simon Bar-Jonah, for flesh and blood has not revealed this to you, but My Father in heaven. And I say to you, you are Peter, and upon this rock I will build My Church, and the gates of hell shall not prevail against it. And I will give you the keys of the kingdom of heaven; and whatever you shall bind on earth shall be bound in heaven, and whatever you shall loose on earth shall be loosed in heaven."

By these words Jesus promised to make Peter the head of His Church. Keys are a symbol of power. Jesus meant that Peter was to have power to rule His Church.

Peter was the first Pope of the Holy Catholic Church. He was the head, on earth, of the religion founded by Jesus Christ Himself, the only True Religion. Peter was the first of the long line of popes that have succeeded each other ever since the time of Christ to rule God's Church.

After this Jesus began to tell His apostles what things were to come upon Him before many months. He said, "The Son of Man must suffer many things, and be rejected by the elders and chief priests and Scribes, and be put to death, and on the third day He will rise again."

Peter took Jesus aside and told Him that He would not be put to death. But our Lord told Peter that his thoughts were still too worldly. The kingdom of which He was to be the head would not be an earthly one.

Jesus is transfigured and Moses and Elijah come to talk with Him,
as Peter, James, and John look on.

36. THE TRANSFIGURATION

ABOUT six days later, Jesus and His apostles were passing by a high hill. It was our Lord's custom to leave the apostles, especially in the evening, and go to a quiet place to pray. Jesus left the apostles at the foot of the hill and took with Him only Peter, James and John. They went up the hill to pray.

While Jesus was praying, a great change came over Him. His face began to shine as brightly as the sun, and His garments became whiter than snow. The three apostles saw their Lord with all this glory beaming from Him.

And they saw two men talking with Jesus. These were Moses and Elijah, who had come down from heaven to meet Jesus. They represented the Law and the prophets that had announced the coming of Jesus. Now they spoke with Him of the death that He was to die in Jerusalem.

Scarcely knowing what he was saying, Peter spoke, "Master, it is good for us to be here! If You wish, let us set up three tents here, one for You, one for Moses, and one for Elijah!"

While Peter was speaking, a bright cloud came over them all. The three apostles felt a great fear as they found themselves in the cloud. Out of the cloud the apostles heard a voice saying, "This is My beloved Son, in whom I am well pleased; hear Him."

As the apostles heard this voice, they fell down upon their faces on the ground in great fear. And Jesus came and touched them, saying, "Arise, and do not be afraid."

When they looked up, the bright cloud had passed away, and Jesus was standing there alone. They walked together down the mountain, and Jesus said to them, "Do not tell to any man what you have seen, until the Son of Man is risen from the dead."

Our Lord had allowed Peter and James and John to see some of His glory to strengthen their faith in Him.

Peter extracts the half-shekel from the fish
which Jesus told him would be there.

37. THE TEMPLE DUES

A T THE time of Jesus, there was a yearly dues or tax for the upkeep of the magnificent Temple in Jerusalem. Each adult male Jew was required to pay the sum of a half-shekel for this purpose.

One day, Jesus and His disciples arrived at Capernaum. The collectors of the half-shekel approached Peter and said, "Does your Master not pay the half-shekel?"

"Yes," he replied, and went into the house. But before he could speak, Jesus said, "Simon, what is your opinion? From whom do the kings of the earth take tribute? From their sons or from foreigners?"

"From foreigners," replied Peter.

"Well then, the sons are exempt," Jesus said. "However, so as not to offend these people, go to the lake and cast a hook. Take the first fish that bites, open its mouth and there you will find a shekel. Take it and give it to them for Me and for you."

Peter did as Jesus said and found the silver coin. Filled with wonder and joy, he came back and showed the coin to Jesus. Then he paid the temple dues with it.

By "sons" Jesus meant Himself and the disciples who were His brothers and sons of the same Father. So they were exempt from the Temple tax. In these words Jesus declared that He was the Son of God.

Jesus places His arms about the little children and blesses them.

38. JESUS AND LITTLE CHILDREN

ONE day, Jesus was instructing the people, and mothers began bringing their little children to Him. They wanted Him to place His holy hands on them and to pray for them.

When the disciples saw the mothers coming with the children, they were upset. They did not think Jesus should be disturbed in this way. So they began to turn the mothers and children aside.

The mothers and children were disappointed. They had come with such great hopes. Now they could not even speak to the Master.

At this point, Jesus caught sight of the mothers and children, and of the disciples turning them away. He became indignant and rebuked the disciples for their action.

Jesus said to them, "Let the little children come to Me, for of such is the kingdom of God. I assure you that whoever does not accept the kingdom of God like a little child shall not take part in it."

Jesus then put His arms about the children and began to bless them.

From this we learn many important lessons. No matter how old we may be, we should have clean hearts full of simple trust and faith in God, like the children that Jesus told us to imitate. We should also have special care for children and love them as Jesus loved them.

Jesus says it would be better for one who scandalizes a child to have a great millstone hung around his neck.

39. AVOIDING SCANDAL

ON another occasion, as Jesus and the apostles were going to Capernaum, the apostles began to argue among themselves about which of them would be the greatest in the kingdom of heaven.

On their arrival, Jesus asked them what they had been talking about on the way. They were ashamed to tell Him. But Jesus knew. And sitting down, he called the apostles and said to them, "If any man wishes to be first, he shall be last of all, and servant of all."

Jesus took a little child in His arms and held him up before all His apostles and said to them , "Unless you become as little children, you will not enter into the kingdom of heaven. Whoever, therefore, humbles himself as this little child, he is the greatest in the kingdom of heaven.

"Whoever receives one such little child for My sake, receives Me. But whoever causes one of these little ones who believe in Me to sin, it would be better for him to have a great millstone hung around his neck and to be drowned in the depths of the sea.

"See that you do not despise one of these little ones; for I tell you, their angels in heaven always behold the face of My Father in heaven. For the Son of Man came to save what was lost. It is not the will of your Father in heaven that a single one of these little ones should perish."

Jesus and His disciples during His public ministry.

40. THE MISSION OF THE APOSTLES

ONE day two blind men followed Jesus, crying out, "Have pity on us, Son of David!" And Jesus said to them, "Do you believe that I can do this to you?" They answered Him, "Yes, Lord."

Then He touched their eyes, saying, "Let it be done to you according to your faith."

And their eyes were opened. And they went out and spread His fame abroad throughout all that district.

Jesus was going about all the towns and villages of Galilee, teaching in the synagogues, and preaching the Gospel of the kingdom of heaven, and healing the sick people who were brought to Him. But seeing the crowds, He was moved with pity for them, because they were sad and wandering like sheep without a shepherd.

Then Jesus said to His disciples, "The harvest indeed is abundant, but the laborers are few. Pray therefore the Lord of the harvest to send forth laborers into His harvest . . . Behold, I am sending you forth like sheep in the midst of wolves. Be therefore wise as serpents, and simple as doves. But beware of men; for they will deliver you up to councils, and scourge you in their synagogues, and you will be brought before governors and kings for My sake, for a witness to them and to the Gentiles. But when they deliver you up, do not be anxious how or what you are to speak; for what you are to speak will be given you in that hour. For it is not you who are speaking, but the Spirit of your Father who speaks through you . . . You will be hated by all for My name's sake; but he who has persevered to the end will be saved."

In these words Jesus showed His power as God and Head of the Church of which He was the founder. He sent forth His apostles because He wished to prove before the whole world that He had full authority from God, and could give and exercise it as He pleased, in His own Person or through others. He wished to make known that He had founded a new means of giving His grace, that is, through His apostles and through the priests who would follow them. He gave them full authority and power for the exercise of the apostolic office. He taught them that their mission was to comfort and benefit people, and to lead them to eternal happiness. In spite of persecutions, His Church would last until the end of time, as He promised, because it was the work of God.

After this Jesus sent out His twelve apostles to different parts in Galilee to preach in His name to the people. He sent them forth in pairs, two of them together, so that they could help each other. He gave them power to heal the sick and to cast out evil spirits from men. He said to them, "He that hears you, hears Me; and he that hears Me, hears Him who sent Me."

The Samaritan dresses the wounds of the injured man.

41. THE GOOD SAMARITAN

AT THAT time one of the Scribes — men who wrote copies of the books of the Old Testament, studied them, and taught them — came to Jesus and asked Him a question, "Master, what must I do to gain eternal life?"

Jesus said to the Scribe, "What is written in the Law?"

The Scribe answered, "You shall love the Lord your God with your whole heart, and with your whole soul, and with your whole strength, and with your whole mind; and your neighbor as yourself."

Jesus said to him, "You have answered right; do this and you shall have everlasting life."

But the man was not satisfied. He asked another question, "And who is my neighbor?"

To answer this question, Jesus told the story of "The Good Samaritan." He said, "A certain man was going down the lonely road from Jerusalem to Jericho; and he fell among robbers. They stripped him of all that he had and beat him, and then went away, leaving him almost dead. It happened that a certain priest was going down that road; and when he saw the man lying there, he passed by on the other side. And a Levite also, when he came to the place and saw the man, he too went by on the other side. But a certain Samaritan, as he was going down, came where this man was; and as soon as he saw him, he felt pity for him. He came to the man and dressed his wounds, pouring oil and wine into them. Then he lifted him up, set him on his own beast of burden, and walked beside him to an inn. There he took care of him all night. The next morning he took out from his purse two coins and gave them to the keeper of the inn and said, 'Take care of him; and if you need to spend more than this, do so; and when I come again, I will pay it to you.'

"Which one of these three do you think showed himself a neighbor to the man who fell among the robbers?"

The Scribe said, "The one who showed mercy to him."

Then Jesus said to him, "Go and do in like manner."

By this parable Jesus showed that our neighbor, no matter who he may be, is the one who needs the help that we can give him. We must imitate the Samaritan in his exercise of the law of charity if we wish to possess eternal life. Regardless of a man's creed or country or social standing, we believe that the image of God is engraved upon his soul; the Blood of Jesus was shed for his salvation. He is a child of God and our brother, and he is destined to eternal glory.

Jesus is the Good Samaritan who stops by the way to care for and help souls fallen into sin and stripped of the garments of grace by Satan. In His mercy Jesus restores the sinner to God's favor and spiritual health, so that he may continue along the road to heaven.

Jesus answers Martha's complaint, "Only one thing is needful. Mary has chosen the best part, and it will not be taken away from her."

42. JESUS WITH MARTHA AND MARY

WHILE Jesus was teaching in Jerusalem, He often went out of the city to the village of Bethany, on the Mount of Olives. There He stayed with the family of Martha, her sister Mary, and their brother Lazarus. These were friends of Jesus, and He loved to be with them.

One day, while Jesus was at their house, Mary sat at the feet of Jesus, listening to His words. Martha was busy with work and full of cares. She went back and forth, preparing food and arranging the house. When Martha saw Mary, she said to Jesus, "Lord, is it right that my sister should leave me to do the work alone? Tell her to help me."

But Jesus said to her, "Martha, Martha, you are anxious and troubled about many things; and yet only one thing is needful. Mary has chosen the best part, and it will not be taken away from her."

Jesus told Martha that it was more important to take care of the soul than the body. Jesus often taught that people should not always be thinking of money and other worldly things. He said, "Do not lay up for yourselves treasures on earth, where rust and moth consume, and where thieves break in and steal; but lay up for yourselves treasures in heaven, where neither rust nor moth consumes, nor thieves break in and steal . . . Do not be anxious for your life, what you shall eat; nor yet for your body, what you shall put on, for your Father knows that you need all these things. But seek first the kingdom of God and His justice, and all these things shall be given you besides."

"If anyone wishes to come after Me, let him deny himself, and take up his cross, and follow Me. For what does it profit a man, if he gain the whole world, but suffer the loss of his own soul? Or what will a man give in exchange for his soul? For the Son of Man is to come with His angels in the glory of His Father, and then He will render to everyone according to his conduct."

Jesus says to those who brought an adulteress to Him, "Let the one among you who has never sinned throw the first stone."

43. THE ADULTERESS

EARLY one morning, Jesus went to the Temple and the people started coming to Him. Sitting down in the Temple precinct, He began to teach them.

The scribes and Pharisees came and brought a woman before Him. They said, "Master, this woman has been caught in the act of adultery. According to the Law, Moses commanded such women to be stoned to death. What do You have to say about her?"

They were asking this question to trap Jesus, so that they could accuse Him of something.

Jesus stooped down and began to write with His finger in the dust of the ground. When they continued to ask their question, Jesus straightened up and said to them, "Let the one among you who has never sinned throw the first stone at her."

Then Jesus stooped down again and continued writing with His finger on the ground. One by one the audience drifted away, beginning with the elders. This left Jesus alone with the woman, who continued to stand before Him.

"Where are they all?" He asked. "Has no one condemned you?"

"No one, Sir," she said.

"Neither do I condemn you," said Jesus to her. "Go home and do not sin again."

*The Prodigal Son returns home and is met and welcomed
by his happy father.*

44. THE PRODIGAL SON

THERE was a man who had two sons. The younger one said to his father, "Father, give me my share of the property." And when the father had given him his share, the young man went to a distant country and spent the money foolishly.

And when he had spent all he had, there was a severe famine in that country, and he became hungry. So he got a job as a keeper of pigs. For food he had to be satisfied with what was left over after the pigs had finished eating.

When he came to his right mind, he said to himself, "How many of my father's servants have enough to eat and to spare, and here I am dying of hunger. I will go back to my father, and say to him, 'Father, I have sinned against heaven and against you, and am no longer worthy to be called your son. Let me be a hired servant in your house.'"

So he started homeward. But while he was still a long way off, the father saw him. He ran to meet him, and kissed him and held him tightly. "Father, I have done wrong in the sight of God, and of you!" cried the boy; "I am not worthy to be called your son."

But the father said to his servants, "Bring out the best clothes and put them on him, and put a ring on his finger, and shoes on his feet, and let us feast and be glad today, for this son of mine was dead and is alive again. He was lost and is found!" And they had a great feast.

But the elder son had been out in the field all the while, and now he came near to the house.

"How many years have I obeyed you," said the elder son to his father, "and you never even gave me a young goat to eat with my friends. But now that this rascal comes back after wasting all your money, you give a grand feast for him!"

"Son," said his father, "you are always with me, and all that I have is yours. Let us be happy and rejoice, for your brother was dead, and has come to life; he was lost, and is found."

The stone is removed from the tomb and Jesus calls out, "Lazarus, come forth!" And Lazarus comes out from the tomb, with hands and feet still wrapped with linen.

45. LAZARUS RAISED FROM THE DEAD

MARTHA and Mary sent word to Jesus that Lazarus, their brother, was sick. Two days later Lazarus died.

Now Martha heard that Jesus was coming, and she went to meet Him.

Jesus said to her, "Your brother shall be alive again."

"I know that he will be alive again in the resurrection, at the last day," said Martha.

Jesus said, "I am the resurrection and the life; he who believes in Me, even if he die, shall live; and whoever lives and believes in Me, shall never die. Do you believe this?"

"Yes, Master," said Martha, "I believe that You are the Christ, the Son of God."

Now Mary came and bowed in sorrow at the feet of Jesus. And seeing her tears and the grief of friends who stood there, Jesus wept.

And He came to the tomb, which was a cave with a stone at the entrance.

"Take away the stone," said Jesus.

"But, Master!" cried Martha, "Lazarus has been dead and in the tomb for the past four days!"

Jesus said, "Have I not said to you, 'Believe, and you will see the glory of God'?"

So they moved away the stone. And Jesus turned to God in prayer. "Father, I thank You that You have heard Me. I know that You always hear Me; yet I say this because of the people standing here, so that they may believe that You sent Me."

Then He called with a loud voice, "Lazarus, come forth!"

And the man who had been dead came out, though his hands and feet were still wrapped with linen. Jesus said to those who were near, "Unbind him, and set him free."

Many of the Jews believed in Him.

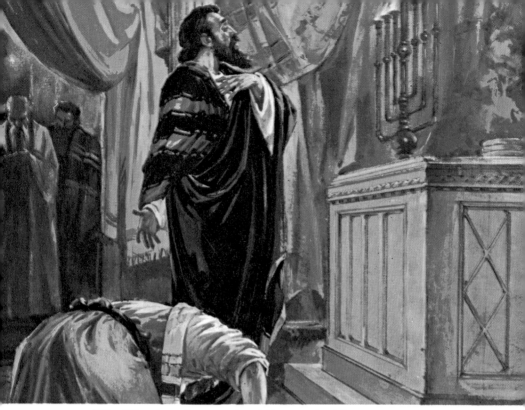

The Pharisee is proud, while the Publican is very humble.

46. THE PHARISEE AND THE PUBLICAN

JESUS taught that God loves humility. He once told this parable:

"Two men went up to the Temple to pray, the one a Pharisee and the other a publican. The Pharisee stood and began to pray, 'O God, I thank You that I am not like the rest of men, robbers, dishonest, and unjust men like this publican. I fast twice a week. I give alms to the Temple.'

"But the publican stood at the back, far off. He would not so much as lift up his eyes to heaven, but kept striking his breast, saying, 'O God, be merciful to me, a sinner!'

"I say to you, this man went back to his home having his sins forgiven rather than the other, for everyone who exalts himself shall be humbled, and he who humbles himself shall be exalted."

Jesus says, "Receive your sight."

47. THE BLIND MAN

JESUS with His disciples drew near to Jericho. Just outside the city, at the gate, was sitting a blind man, begging This man heard the noise of the crowd and he asked what it meant. They said to him, "Jesus of Nazareth is passing by." As soon as he heard this, he began to cry out, "Jesus, Son of David, have mercy on me!"

Jesus, hearing his cry, said, "Call the man to Me!" When the blind man reached Him, Jesus said to him, "What do you wish Me to do for you?"

He answered, "Lord, that I may see."

Then Jesus touched his eyes and said, "Receive your sight; your faith has made you well."

At once sight came to his eyes and he followed Jesus, while all the people who saw the miracle gave thanks to God.

Jesus says to the rich young man, "Come, follow Me."

48. THE RICH YOUNG MAN

A YOUNG man once said to Jesus, "Good Master, what shall I do to gain eternal life?" Jesus answered, "You know the commandments."

The young man said, "All these I have kept ever since I was a child."

And Jesus loved him, and said, "If you want to be perfect, sell all that you have, and give to the poor, and you shall have treasure in heaven; and come, follow Me."

But when the young man heard this, he turned and went away very sad, for he was very rich.

Then Peter said, "Behold, we have left all and followed You."

Jesus answered him, "Amen, I say to you, there is no one who has left house, or parents, or brothers, or wife, or children, for the sake of the kingdom of God, who shall not receive much in the present time, and in the age to come life everlasting."

The Good Shepherd finds the sheep which has strayed.

49. THE GOOD SHEPHERD

JESUS said, "I am the good shepherd. The good shepherd lays down his life for his sheep. But the hireling, who is not a shepherd, whose own the sheep are not, sees the wolf coming and leaves the sheep and flees. And the wolf snatches and scatters the sheep . . . I am the good shepherd, and I know mine and mine know Me, even as the Father knows Me and I know the Father; and I lay down My life for My sheep. And other sheep I have that are not of this fold. Them also I must bring, and they shall hear My voice, and there shall be one fold and one shepherd."

"What man of you having a hundred sheep, and losing one of them, does not leave the ninety-nine in the desert, and go after that which is lost, until he finds it? And when he has found it, he lays it upon his shoulders rejoicing. Even so, there will be joy in heaven over one sinner who repents, more than over ninety-nine just who have no need of repentance."

The mother of James and John asks Jesus to place her sons on his right and his left hand in His Kingdom.

50. THE MOTHER OF JAMES AND JOHN

AS JESUS was about to go up to Jerusalem, He took the twelve disciples aside and spoke to them as they walked along. "We are now going up to Jerusalem, and the Son of Man will be handed over to the chief priests and the scribes—and they will condemn Him to death. They will hand Him over to the heathen to ridicule and scourge and crucify Him. And on the third day He will rise again."

Then the mother of the apostles James and John, the sons of Zebedee, came up to Jesus accompanied by her sons. She obviously wanted to make a request. So Jesus asked her, "What is it you want?"

She said to Him, "Promise that these two sons of mine may sit one at Your right hand and the other at Your left in Your kingdom."

Jesus looked at the two disciples and said, "You do not know what it is you are asking. Can you two drink what I have to drink?"

"We can," they said.

"Very well," Jesus replied, "you shall drink My cup. But as for seats at My right hand and My left, these are not Mine to grant. They belong to those for whom My Father has planned it."

The other ten apostles on learning about this became indignant at the two brothers. Jesus then called all of them together and said, "You know how those who exercise authority among the Gentiles lord it over them; their great ones make their importance felt. But it cannot be like that with you.

"Whoever among you wants to be great must become the servant of you all—just as the Son of Man has not come to be served but to serve, and to give His life to set others free."

Jesus says to Zacchaeus, "Hurry, Zacchaeus, because I must visit at your house today.

51. ZACCHAEUS THE PUBLICAN

ONE day Jesus was passing through the city of Jericho, one of the largest cities of Israel. It was the center of one of the tax collecting districts and many tax collectors were employed there.

The chief tax collector was a wealthy man named Zacchaeus. He had learned of Jesus' coming and was anxious to see what kind of person He was. He went down to the roadside where Jesus was coming by. But there were so many people and he was so short that he could not see Jesus.

Zacchaeus ran ahead and climbed a sycamore tree to watch Jesus as He passed by.

When Jesus reached the spot He looked up and called to Zacchaeus to come down. "Hurry, Zacchaeus, because I must visit your house today."

Zacchaeus hurried down and welcomed him joyfully. But the Pharisees complained when they saw what was happening. "He has gone to stay at the house of a sinner," they said.

But Zacchaeus said to Jesus, "Look, Sir, I am going to give half my property to the poor, and if I have cheated anybody I will pay him back four times the amount."

"Today salvation has come to this house," Jesus said to him, "because this man too is a son of Abraham; for the Son of Man has come to seek out and save what was lost."

In Holy Communion Jesus visits our soul and salvation comes to us through His divine life of grace. Thus we are enabled to live a life pleasing to God.

Jesus enters Jerusalem in triumph and the people shout,
"Hosanna to the Son of David."

52. ENTRY INTO JERUSALEM

NOW the chief priests and elders held a meeting of the High Council. "What are we to do about this man and His miracles?" they said. "If we let Him go on this way, all the world will believe in Him, and the Romans will come and destroy our holy place and our people. It is better for one man to die than our whole nation."

After this Jesus could not go about publicly among the Jews. He went out into the desert with His disciples.

But when it was time for the Passover feast, He said to them, "We are going up to Jerusalem, and the Son of Man will be betrayed into the hands of the chief priests and elders, who will condemn Him to death, and give Him over to the Gentiles. They will mock Him and scourge Him and crucify Him. But the third day He will rise from the dead."

The disciples did not understand what Jesus was saying.

On the way, as they came to a village near Jerusalem, He said to two of His disciples, "Go into yonder village, and you will see a donkey tied there, and a colt with her. Untie them and bring them to Me."

So the disciples went and found the donkey with the colt; they put their cloaks over her back, and Jesus rode on the donkey into Jerusalem.

And great crowds of people went along with Him; some threw their cloaks on the road, and some cut branches from the trees and spread them in His path. And all the people, those who went before Him and those who followed Him, shouted, "Hosanna to the Son of David. Blessed is He who comes as King in the name of the Lord! Glory in the highest!"

And some of the Pharisees from the crowds said to Him, "Master, rebuke Your disciples."

Jesus answered, "I tell you that if these keep silence, the stones will cry out."

In the daytime Jesus taught in the Temple, and at night He went out and stayed on the Mount of Olives.

Jesus washes the feet of His apostles.

53. WASHING OF THE FEET AT THE LAST SUPPER

BEFORE the Passover, Jesus said to Peter and John, "When you enter the city, a man will show you a large upper room furnished; there make ready the Passover."

On Thursday afternoon, Jesus and His apostles walked out of Bethany together into the city. They went into the house and went upstairs to the large room, where they found the supper all ready.

Jesus took off His outer robe and tied around His waist a long towel. He poured water into a basin and began to wash the feet of the apostles. When He came to Peter, Peter said to Him, "Lord, You shall never wash my feet!"

"If I do not wash you," said Jesus, "then you shall have no part with Me."

Then Peter said, "Lord, wash not my feet only, but also my hands and my head!"

But Jesus said to them, "If I, the Lord and Master have washed your feet, you also ought to wash the feet of one another. For I have given you an example, that as I have done to you, so you also should do. No servant is greater than his master."

While Jesus was talking, He became very sad and said, "One of you will betray Me."

Then all the apostles looked around at one another wondering who was the one that Jesus meant. John asked Jesus, "Lord, who is it?"

Jesus answered, "It is he for whom I shall dip the bread and give it to him." And when He had dipped the bread, He gave it to Judas Iscariot. And Jesus said to him, "Do quickly what you are going to do."

Judas at once went out, for he saw that his plan was known, and it had to be carried out immediately.

After blessing a piece of bread, Jesus breaks it and gives it to His apostles, saying, "Take and eat; this is My Body."

54. THE INSTITUTION OF THE HOLY EUCHARIST AT THE LAST SUPPER

NOW the moment for which Jesus had waited so long had come. He kept the promise He had made in the synagogue at Capernaum. He took a piece of bread, blessed it, and broke it. Then He gave it to the apostles and said, "Take and eat; this is My Body."

Then He took a cup with wine in it, blessed it in the same way and said, "All of you drink of this; for this is My Blood of the new covenant, which is being shed for many unto the forgiveness of sins . . . Do this in remembrance of Me."

Our Lord changed bread and wine into His Body and Blood and offered Himself to God. This was a sacrifice. At the same time He told the apostles that He would die on the next day. This would be the bloody sacrifice. But Jesus wanted this unbloody sacrifice to continue on earth till the end of time. When He told the apostles to do as He had done, He made them priests who could offer this sacrifice. They could pass this power on to their successors. After our Lord returned to heaven, the apostles continued to offer this Eucharistic Sacrifice. They ordained other priests. In this way Jesus gave us the priesthood and the Mass.

Finally, Jesus gave the apostles His last instructions. He said, "A new commandment I give you, that you love one another: that as I have loved you, you also love one another. By this will all men know that you are My disciples, if you have love for one another."

Jesus said, "I am the vine, and you are the branches. He who abides in Me, and I in him, he bears much fruit; for without Me you can do nothing. If anyone does not abide in Me, he shall be cast outside as the branch and wither; and they shall gather them up and cast them into the fire, and they shall burn. If you abide in Me, and if My words abide in you, ask whatever you will and it shall be done to you."

Jesus with His apostles at the Last Supper.

55. THE HIGH-PRIESTLY PRAYER OF JESUS AT THE LAST SUPPER

RAISING His eyes to heaven, Jesus said, "Father, the hour has come! Glorify Your Son, that Your Son may glorify You, even as You have given Him power over all flesh, in order that to all You have given Him He may give everlasting life. Now this is everlasting life, that they may know You, the only true God, and Him whom You have sent, Jesus Christ. I have glorified You on earth; I have accomplished the work that You have given Me to do. And now do You, Father, glorify Me with Yourself, with the glory that I had with You before the world existed...

"Holy Father, keep in Your name those whom You have given Me, that they may be one even as We are... I have given them Your word; and the world hated them, because they are not of the world, even as I am not of the world. I do not pray that You take them out of the world, but that You keep them from evil... Even as You have sent me into the world, so I also have sent them into the world. And for them I sanctify Myself, that they also may be sanctified in truth.

"Yet not for these only do I pray, but for those also who through their word are to believe in Me, that all may be one, even as You, Father, in Me and I in You; that they also may be one in US, that the world may believe that You have sent Me.

"Father, I will that where I am, they also whom You have given Me may be with Me; in order that they may behold My glory, which You have given Me, because You have loved Me before the creation of the world. Just Father, the world has not known You, but I have known You, and these have known that You have sent Me. And I have made known to them Your name; and will make it known, in order that the love with which You have loved Me may be in them, and I in them."

And after singing a hymn, they went out to Mount Olivet. Then Jesus said to them, "You will all be scandalized this night because of Me . . . But after I have risen, I will go before you into Galilee."

Peter said to Jesus, "Even though all shall be scandalized because of You, I will never be scandalized."

Jesus said to him, "Amen I say to you, this very night, before a cock crows, you will deny Me three times."

Peter said to Him, "Even if I should have to die with You, I will not deny You!"

And all the disciples said the same thing.

Jesus prays while the apostles sleep.

56. THE AGONY IN THE GARDEN

JESUS took with Him Peter, James, and John, and went into the garden of Gethsemane. He said, "My soul is sad, even unto death. Wait here and watch with Me."

He went a little farther among the trees and fell down upon the ground and cried out, "Father, if it is possible, let this cup pass away from Me; yet not as I will, but as You will."

Large drops of sweat like blood, caused by His suffering, fell from His face. Then He went to His apostles and found them asleep. Waking them, He said, "Could you not watch one hour with Me? Watch and pray, that you may not enter into temptation."

He went a second time into the orchard, and He fell on His knees and prayed again, saying, "My Father, if this cup cannot pass away unless I drink it, Your will be done."

Again He found the apostles sleeping. He went back and prayed a third time. And an angel came and gave Him strength.

Judas says, "Hail Rabbi," and kisses Jesus.

57. JUDAS BETRAYS JESUS

ONCE more Jesus went to the three apostles and said to them, "Behold, the hour is at hand, when the Son of Man will be betrayed into the hands of sinners. Rise up, let us be going. See, the traitor is here!"

Judas told the servants of the high priest, "Whomever I kiss, that is He; seize Him, and lead Him safely away." And when he came to the orchard, he went straight up to Jesus and said, "Hail, Rabbi!" and kissed Him.

And Jesus said to him, "Friend, why have you come? Judas, do you want to betray Me with a kiss?"

The servants of the high priest seized Jesus and bound Him and led Him first to the home of the high priest. They presented Him to Annas who was the father-in-law of Caiaphas, the high priest. Then Annas sent Him to Caiaphas.

Jesus says He is God, and the High Priest tears his garments.

58. JESUS BEFORE CAIAPHAS

THE high priest Caiaphas asked Jesus about His disciples and His teaching. Jesus said, "I have spoken openly to the world. Ask the people to whom I have spoken." At once one of the servants struck Jesus in the face.

The priests and the Jewish court were looking for people who would tell lies about Jesus. But Jesus did not say a word to defend Himself.

At last, the high priest said, "I command You by the living God, tell us whether You are the Christ, the Son of God?"

To this Jesus answered, "I am. And you shall see the Son of Man sitting at the right hand of God and coming upon the clouds of heaven."

The high priest tore his garments in anger and said, "He has blasphemed. What do you think?"

And all answered, "He is guilty of death!" Then they spat in His face and struck Him.

Peter weeps bitterly after denying Jesus.

59. PETER DENIES JESUS

WHILE Jesus was before the high priest, Peter remained in the courtyard and warmed himself at the fire. A serving maid in the house said to him, "You were one of those men with this Jesus of Nazareth!"

Peter answered her, "Woman, I do not know the man; I do not know what you are talking about." Another maid asked him the same question, and he denied the second time.

Soon a man came by who looked at Peter and heard him speak. He said, "You are surely one of this man's disciples, for your speech shows that you came from Galilee."

Then Peter began to swear, declaring that he did not know the man of whom they were speaking.

At that moment the loud, shrill crowing of a cock was heard, and Peter remembered what Jesus had said, "Before a cock crows, you will deny Me three times."

Then Peter went out into the dark street and wept bitterly.

When Pilate looks at Jesus, he says, "Are You a King?"

60. JESUS BEFORE PILATE

IT WAS early morning when the rulers of the Jews brought Jesus to Pilate. Pilate came out to them and asked them, "What charge do you bring against this man?"

They answered, "If He were not an evildoer, we would not have brought Him to you."

Pilate did not wish to be troubled and he said, "Take Him away and judge Him by your own law!"

The Jews said to Pilate, "We are not allowed to put any man to death. We have found this man teaching evil and telling men not to pay taxes to the Roman Emperor, Caesar, and saying that He Himself is Christ, a King."

Then Pilate went into his courtroom and sent for Jesus. When he looked at Jesus, he said, "Are You the King of the Jews? Your own people have brought You to me. What have You done?"

Jesus said to him, "My kingdom is not of this world. If My kingdom were of this world, My followers would have fought that I might not be delivered to the Jews. But, My kingdom is not from here."

Pilate said, "Are You a King, then?"

Jesus answered him, "I am a King. This is why I was born, and why I have come into the world, to bear witness to the truth. Everyone who is of the truth hears My voice."

Pilate said to Him, "What is truth?"

Then, without waiting for an answer, Pilate went out to the rulers and the crowd and said, "I find no evil in this man."

But the crowd cried out, "He stirs up the people everywhere, from Galilee even to this place."

When Pilate heard that Jesus had come from Galilee, he sent Jesus to Herod, the ruler of Galilee, who was then in the city.

The soldiers mock Jesus.

61. JESUS IS SCOURGED

HEROD'S soldiers mocked Jesus, dressed Him in a white robe, as if He were a fool, and sent Him back to Pilate.

Then Pilate, to please the people, gave them what they asked. He set free Barabbas. Pilate thought that if he had Jesus scourged, the leaders of the Jews would be satisfied and that he could then free Jesus. He gave Jesus to the soldiers to be scourged. The soldiers stripped Him of His garments and beat Him with rods till His body was covered with blood.

Because Jesus had been spoken of as a King, the soldiers who beat Him made a crown of thorns and put it on His head. They put on Him an old purple robe, the color of kings, and bowing down before Him, they called out to Him, "Hail, King of the Jews!" They mocked Him, spat upon Him, and struck Him.

62. BEHOLD THE MAN

HOPING to awaken some pity for Jesus, Pilate brought Him out to the people, with the crown of thorns and the purple robe upon Him. Pilate said, "Behold the man! I bring Him forth to you, that you may know that I find no guilt in Him."

When the chief priests and their servants saw Jesus, they cried out, "Crucify Him! We have a law, and according to this law He must die, because He made Himself the Son of God." *Pilate presents Jesus to the people.*

When Pilate heard this, he feared the more and wanted all the more to release Jesus. But when the chief priests saw that he was hesitating, they again cried out, "If you release this man, you are not a friend of Caesar's. Anyone that makes himself a king opposes Caesar."

Then Pilate called for a basin of water. He washed his hands before the Jews and said, "I am innocent of this man's blood."

But the leaders of the Jews shouted, "Let His blood be on us and on our children. Away with Him! Crucify Him!"

"Would you have me crucify your King?" asked Pilate.

"He is not our King; we will not have Him for our King," cried the wicked men.

Then Pilate saw it was no use to try to save Jesus, and because he was a coward and was afraid of the people, he said, "Take Him then, and crucify Him yourselves."

Then Pilate turned Jesus over to the Roman soldiers.

Jesus falls under the weight of the cross.

63. ON THE ROAD TO CALVARY

THE Roman soldiers then took Jesus and beat Him again most cruelly and prepared to lead Him out of the city to the place of death. This was a place called "Golgotha" in the Jewish language, "Calvary" in that of the Romans; both words meaning "The Skull Place."

As was the custom, Jesus was to carry His own cross to Calvary. He received it and tenderly pressed it to His Heart. Though He received the cross from the hand of His Father in heaven, it was really we who placed it upon His shoulder.

Tired and broken with pain of body and grief of soul, Jesus struggled forward with the cross. His body swayed beneath the heavy load and He fell to the ground. By His fall, He atoned for our pride and gave us the grace to rise again after falling into sin.

JESUS MEETS HIS MOTHER

Sorrow pierced the loving soul of Mary when she caught sight of Jesus, her beloved Son, now so changed and deformed that she could scarcely recognize Him. When Jesus met her so sorrowful, His own Heart was torn with pain. And Mary felt all His pain together with Him. That dear Mother of Sorrows gave Him up to die for our redemption.

✠

JESUS IS HELPED BY SIMON

The soldiers kicked and dragged Jesus along, and lest He should die on the way, they forced a stranger, Simon of Cyrene, to help Him carry the cross. But, after the grateful, loving glance of Jesus, Simon found his duty a pleasure. Since Christ calls to suffering those whom He loves, we ought to beg for Simon's privilege to carry our cross of pain bravely for His sake.

JESUS AND VERONICA

Veronica lovingly wiped the sad face of Jesus, stained with blood and spittle and sweat. Tears sprang from His eyes at the sight of this act of kindness. Upon her linen cloth He left the half-dying expression of His face, but upon her heart He imprinted His look of grateful love. The image of the sorrowful Face of Jesus should help us remember the undying love of the Savior.

✠

JESUS SPEAKS TO THE WOMEN

With the soldiers, a great crowd of people went out of the city. Some of them were enemies of Jesus, glad to see Him suffer; others were friends. He turned to a group of women who were weeping as they saw Him going out to die, and said to them, "Daughters of Jerusalem, do not weep for Me, but weep for yourselves and for your children."

JESUS IS STRIPPED OF HIS GARMENTS

At last the Way of the Cross was finished; Calvary was reached. The soldiers seized Jesus roughly and stripped His garments from His bruised body. The garments adhered to the fresh wounds which He received at the scourging and again painfully tore them open. Jesus wished to be deprived even of His clothing, so that He would have nothing and could give all.

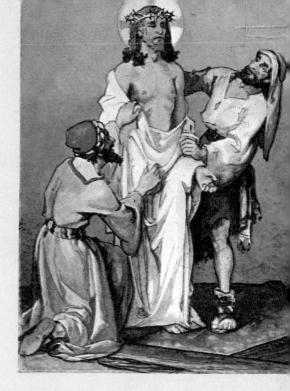

✠

JESUS IS NAILED TO THE CROSS

Into the hands and feet of Jesus the soldiers hammered a heavy nail, while the blood flowed freely. Then they lifted Him up in mid-air. Pilate had this inscription put on the cross: "Jesus of Nazareth, the King of the Jews." The cross was erected as a sign of the justice and mercy of God — an altar on which Jesus offered the bloody sacrifice of the New Testament for the redemption of mankind.

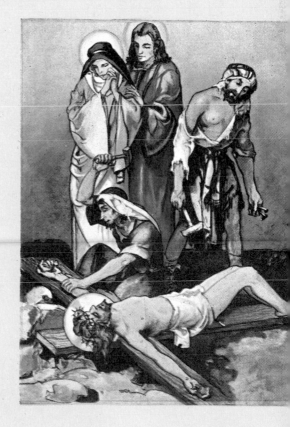

After three hours' agony, Jesus dies on the cross for the salvation of mankind.

64. JESUS DIES ON THE CROSS

JESUS prayed on the cross, "Father, forgive them, for they do not know what they are doing." Two robbers were hung on crosses, one at His right side and the other at His left. One of them said to Jesus, "Lord, remember me when You come into Your kingdom."

And Jesus answered him, "Amen I say to you, this day you shall be with Me in paradise."

Standing by the cross of Jesus was His Mother, and beside her was John, the disciple whom He loved best. Other women besides His Mother were there, His Mother's sister and Mary Magdalene. Jesus wished to give His Mother into the care of John, now that He was leaving her, and He said to her, as He looked from her to John, "Woman, behold your son."

In the middle of the afternoon when Jesus had endured three hours of terrible pain on the cross, He cried out, "My God, My God, why have You forsaken Me?"

After this He spoke again, saying, "I thirst." Someone dipped a sponge into a cup of vinegar and put it upon a reed and gave Him a drink of it.

Then Jesus spoke His last words upon the cross, "It is finished! Father, into Your hands I give My spirit!"

And Jesus died. God died that we sinners might live!

At once a great darkness came over the city of Jerusalem. The earth shook. The rocks split. The tombs opened, and the dead walked about. At that moment the veil of the Temple between the Holy Place and the Holy of Holies was torn apart by unseen hands from the top to the bottom. The Roman officer who had charge of the soldiers around the cross said, "Surely this man was the Son of God."

*Joseph of Arimathea and his friends place the body
of Jesus in the tomb.*

65. THE BURIAL

THE Jews went to Pilate and asked that the bodies be removed so that they would not spoil the Sabbath. Because it was during the feast of the Passover, this Sabbath was a very solemn day. Pilate, therefore, sent some soldiers to be sure that the crucified were dead before their bodies were taken from the crosses. The soldiers killed the two robbers by breaking their bones. But when the soldiers came to Jesus, they found that He was already dead. They did not break His bones, but one of them pierced His side with a lance to be sure that He was dead. John, the apostle, saw the water and blood come from the side of Jesus.

Nicodemus and Joseph were rulers of the Jews and friends of Jesus. Joseph, a rich man who came from the town of Arimathea, went boldly to Pilate and asked that the body of Jesus be given to him. Pilate consented.

Joseph and his friends took the body of Jesus down from the cross and wrapped it in fine linen. And Nicodemus brought some precious spices which they wrapped up with the body. Then they placed the body in Joseph's own new tomb, which was a cave, dug out of the rock, in a garden near the place where the cross stood. And before the entrance of the cave they rolled a great stone.

On the next morning, some of the rulers of the Jews came to Pilate and said, "Sir, we remember how that deceiver said, while He was yet alive, 'After three days I will rise again.' Give orders, therefore, that the tomb be guarded until the third day, or else His disciples may come and steal Him away, and say to the people, 'He has risen from the dead!' "

Pilate said to them, "You have a guard; go, guard it as well as you know how."

Then they placed a seal upon the stone, so that no one might break it; and they set a watch of soldiers at the door.

And the body of Jesus lay in the tomb from the evening of Friday to the dawn of Sunday.

While the guards tremble with fear, Jesus rises from
the dead on the third day.

66. THE RESURRECTION OF JESUS

WHEN the apostles heard that their Master was dead, they returned one by one to Jerusalem. They gathered at the house where they had eaten the Last Supper with Jesus. They were very sad. They had hoped that Jesus would set up His great earthly kingdom at this feast. They also hoped to be important in that kingdom. Now Jesus was dead and with Him all their hopes.

But on Sunday morning, Jesus rose by His own divine power, a glorious Victor, as He had promised. The earth quaked as He came forth from the tomb, and the guards trembled with fear. His body now shone like the sun. The wounds of His hands and feet sparkled like precious jewels. Death was conquered.

In His Resurrection the body of Jesus was glorified by being united again to His glorified Soul. His body took on spiritual qualities: immortality, beauty and glory, freedom and the power to move about with speed and without hindrance. The Divinity shone forth through His glorified body, and floods of joy poured into His Soul and Sacred Heart.

The Resurrection was the crown of the life and work of Jesus as God-Man, because it was the beginning of the glorious life that was due to Him as the Son of God. It was also the reward of His life of suffering.

The Resurrection of Jesus is the strongest proof of His Divinity. The whole truth and meaning of our faith rests upon this greatest of all miracles. If Jesus is the Son of God, His teaching must be true, and the Church which He founded is the Church of the living God. Its sacraments give us the means of salvation by imparting divine grace.

Though it is not mentioned in the Gospels, Jesus surely appeared to His Mother first. He had received from her the life that was now so glorious. Since she shared in all His sorrows and sufferings, it was fitting that she should share in the joy and glory of His triumph.

An angel announces the Resurrection of Jesus to the women.

67. THE WOMEN AT THE TOMB

N SUNDAY morning, some women went very early to the tomb of Jesus. They were bringing fragrant spices to place in the wrappings upon His body.

As soon as Mary Magdalene saw that the tomb was open, she ran quickly to tell the apostles. The other women did not find the body of Jesus. But they saw sitting at each end of the open tomb young men in white garments. One of the angels said to them, "Do not be afraid. You are looking for Jesus of Nazareth, who was crucified. He is not here; He is risen. Go tell His disciples that He will see them in Galilee."

As they went to the city, Jesus appeared and said, "All hail! Go and tell My brethren that I shall see them in Galilee."

Jesus says, "Mary," and she knows that it is the Master.

68. JESUS APPEARS TO MARY MAGDALENE

WHEN Mary Magdalene came back to the tomb, Jesus appeared to her and said, "Mary!" and she knew that He was Jesus, no longer dead, but living. She cried out, "My Master."

The two disciples speak with Jesus without knowing Him.

69. JESUS APPEARS TO TWO DISCIPLES

THAT afternoon, two followers of Jesus were walking out of Jerusalem to a village called Emmaus. While they were talking over the strange happenings of the day, they saw that a stranger was walking beside them. It was Jesus, their risen Lord, but they did not know Him.

They spoke of the way Jesus was crucified, and then said, "But we were hoping that it was He who should redeem Israel, and this is the third day since these things happened."

Then the stranger said to them, "Did not the Christ have to suffer these things before entering into His glory?"

Then, starting with Moses and going through all the Prophets, Jesus explained to them the passages throughout the Scriptures that were about Himself. He talked until they came to the town of Emmaus, where Cleopas and his friends were going to stay. Jesus gave the impression that He meant to go on farther, but they stopped Him with the words, "Do stay with us. It is nearly evening and soon the day will be over."

After Cleopas and his friend prepared some food, the three of them sat down to supper. Jesus blessed the bread and gave it to them. All at once their eyes were opened, and they saw that it was Jesus. While they looked, He vanished out of their sight.

Cleopas and his friend looked at one another and said, "Were not our hearts burning inside us as He talked to us on the road and explained the Scriptures to us?" They got up immediately and returned to Jerusalem, where they found the Eleven apostles and the entire company assembled.

The two disciples were greeted with, "The Lord has been raised! It is true! He has appeared to Simon." Then they recounted what had happened on the road and how they had come to know the Lord in the breaking of bread.

Jesus appears to the apostles and convinces them of His Resurrection.

70. JESUS APPEARS TO THE APOSTLES

ON THAT night ten apostles and other followers of Jesus were together in a room, and the doors were shut. Suddenly Jesus Himself was standing among them. He said, "Peace be to you!"

Some of them were alarmed when they saw Him and thought that He must be a spirit. But He said to them, "Why are you disturbed, and why do doubts arise in your hearts? See My hands and feet, that it is I Myself. Feel Me and see; for a spirit does not have flesh and bones, as you see I have."

And He showed them His hands and His side. They could scarcely believe for the joy of seeing Him again. He said, "Have you anything here to eat?"

They gave Him a piece of broiled fish and some honey, and He ate before them. And He said, "These are the words which I spoke to you while I was yet with you, that all things must be fulfilled that are written in the law of Moses and the Prophets and the Psalms concerning Me." Then He opened their minds, that they might understand the Scriptures.

The apostles were filled with joy. All their sadness left them. Hope came back into their hearts.

Jesus said to them again, "Peace be to you! As the Father has sent Me, I also send you." When He had said this, He breathed upon them and said to them, "Receive the Holy Spirit; whose sins you shall forgive, they are forgiven them; and whose sins you shall retain, they are retained."

In these words Jesus gave the apostles the power to forgive sins, which He had promised them. This power Jesus wished to remain in His Church forever. The apostles passed it on to their successors—the bishops of the Catholic Church. This power is exercised by the priest in the Sacrament of Penance.

Through confession Jesus gives us our spiritual life, peace of conscience, the strength to resist temptation, and a lasting joy.

Jesus turns to Thomas and says, "Bring here your finger, and see My hands; and bring here your hand and put it into My side."

71. UNBELIEVING THOMAS

WHEN Jesus showed Himself to the apostles on the evening of the day of His rising from the dead, only ten of them saw Him, for Thomas was absent. The other disciples said to Thomas, "We have seen the Lord!"

But Thomas said, "Unless I see in His hands the print of the nails, and put my finger into the place of the nails, and put my hand into His side, I will not believe."

A week passed, and on the next Sunday evening the apostles were together again. At this time Thomas was with them. The doors were shut, but suddenly Jesus was seen again standing in the middle of the room. He greeted them as before, "Peace be to you!"

Then He turned to Thomas and said to him, "Bring here your finger, and see My hands; and bring here your hand, and put it into My side; and be not unbelieving, but believing."

And Thomas answered Him, "My Lord and my God!"

Then Jesus said to him, "Because you have seen Me, you have believed. Blessed are they who have not seen, and yet have believed."

The loving way in which Jesus brought Thomas to believe should strengthen in us the spirit of love and confidence, and faith in His Real Presence in the Blessed Sacrament, where we cannot see Him. That faith must be proved by our fervent devotion at Mass, Holy Communion, and by our frequent visits to the Tabernacle.

Jesus proved to the apostles that He had really risen from the dead. After this He appeared to them several times in Jerusalem and in Galilee. Later, when they went out to preach to the world, they could tell how at first they doubted. They could tell how Jesus had convinced them of His Resurrection.

Jesus makes Peter the first Pope.

72. PETER RECEIVES THE PRIMACY

AT ANOTHER time, Jesus appeared to the disciples by the shore and had breakfast with them after a miraculous catch of fish.

After they had finished eating, Jesus said to Peter, "Simon, son of John, do you love Me more than these others do?"

Peter answered, "Yes, Lord, You know I love You."

"Feed My lambs," said Jesus. Then He asked again, "Simon, son of John, do you love Me?"

He replied, "Yes, Lord, You know I love You."

Again Jesus said to him, "Look after My sheep."

Then the third time Jesus said, "Simon, son of John, do you love Me?"

Peter felt very bad that Jesus should ask that question three times. He knew that Jesus was thinking of the three times that he had denied Him on the night of His trial. He answered, "Lord, You know everything; You know I love You."

Jesus said to him, "Feed My sheep."

Jesus did know that Peter loved Him. But He wanted to remind him that He had a work for Peter to do, a work which would demand the sacrifice of his life.

Until now, Peter had only received the promise of the primacy but after this morning meal Jesus conferred the primacy upon him in all its fullness and majesty in the presence of the other apostles.

When He was about to leave His sheep, Jesus appointed Peter as the shepherd in His place. He made him the first Pope of the Catholic Church, whose successor lives in the Vatican.

Jesus ascends into heaven, higher and higher, until a cloud covers Him and the disciples see Him no more.

73. THE ASCENSION

FORTY days after the Resurrection, the followers of Jesus met on a mountain in Galilee. More than five hundred people were gathered at this time; and there Jesus showed Himself to them all. He said to them, "All power in heaven and on earth has been given to Me. Go, therefore, and make disciples of all nations, baptizing them in the name of the Father, and of the Son, and of the Holy Spirit, teaching them to observe all that I have commanded you; and behold, I am with you all days, even unto the consummation of the world."

Then He said to them, "Thus it is written, and thus the Christ should suffer, and should rise again from the dead on the third day; and that repentance and remission of sins should be preached in His name to all the nations, beginning from Jerusalem. And you yourselves are witnesses of these things. And I send forth upon you the promise of My Father. But wait here in the city, until you are clothed with power from on high."

After Jesus had given His last instructions to His apostles and disciples, He lifted up His hands to bless them. And while He was blessing them, He began to rise in the air, higher and higher, until a cloud covered Him and the disciples saw Him no more.

While they were looking up toward heaven, they found two men, like angels, with shining garments, standing by them. These men said, "You men of Galilee, why do you stand looking up into heaven? This Jesus, who has been taken up from you, shall come again from heaven to earth, as you have seen Him go up from earth to heaven!"

Then the disciples were glad. They worshiped their risen Lord Jesus, now gone up to heaven; and they went again to Jerusalem. And there they remained, praising and giving thanks to God, and praying for the coming of the Holy Spirit.

The Holy Spirit comes down upon Mary and the disciples.

74. THE DESCENT OF THE HOLY SPIRIT

AT THE Last Supper Jesus promised to send the Holy Spirit, the Third Person of the Blessed Trinity, to the apostles. The Holy Spirit would strengthen them and be with them always.

After our Lord's ascension into heaven, His apostles and disciples gathered together in an upper room with Mary His Mother, and the holy women. Numbering about one hundred and twenty persons, they spent their time in prayer.

On the tenth day a sound like a mighty wind filled the whole house, and tongues of fire came down upon the head of each one of them. The apostles were filled with the Holy Spirit and began to speak in many strange tongues.

Before the descent of the Holy Spirit, the apostles were afraid. After they had received the Holy Spirit, they were filled with courage and feared nothing. Peter, who had denied his Master three times, came forth with the other apostles, and stood before the crowd. "Men of Israel," he said, "hear these words: Jesus of Nazareth whom you have crucified and put to death by the hands of wicked men, God has raised up. We are all witnesses. And now that He has been taken up into heaven and is at the right of God, He has poured forth His Holy Spirit, which you see and hear, even as He promised."

About three thousand persons were converted by this first sermon. They were baptized and united with the rest of the disciples. And they continued faithfully in the teaching of the apostles and in the Communion of the breaking of the bread and in prayer.

After the feast of Pentecost, the apostles went out into the world and preached Christ crucified. They performed many miracles and converted many people.

The Church, founded by Jesus Christ, will last to the end of time because He sent the Holy Spirit to strengthen, guide, and keep it from error, and because He said, "Behold, I am with you all days, even to the end of the world."

Land of the Bible

S T. JEROME, one of the earliest and greastest students of the Holy Scriptures, remarked that as "we have a better understanding of the Greek historians when we have seen Athens . . . [so] we have a better comprehension of Sacred Scripture when we have seen Judea with our own eyes and contemplated the ruins of its ancient cities."

We hope that the magnificent protographs of sacred shrines and traditional sites identifying actual places traversed by the Son of God while on earth will help bring Bible events to life for all who view them.

The Star of Bethlehem — The silver star of the Grotto of the Nativity marks the spot where Jesus was believed to be born. The Holy Manger can be seen nearby, where Masses are celebrated. This is one of the most ancient of the churches in the world continuously in use, and was built in 325 by Constantine. The word "Bethlehem" means "House of Bread"— *Lk 2:4-7.*

The Golden Gate—Old Jerusalem stands on foundations 200 years old, currently surrounded by a wall almost three miles long. This wall contains 3 towers, and seven open gates. The Golden Gate has been closed for centuries. Its monolithic pillars are said to have been given Solomon by the Queen of Sheba. Jesus is believed to have made His entry into Jerusalem through this gate. It is also called the "Gate of Mercy," and many legends speak of this gate's opening at the "end of days"—*Mk 11:9-11.*

Ancient Synagogue at Capernaum — After rejection in Nazareth, Jesus spent almost two years centering his life around Capernaum, on Lake Galilee's northern shore. Ultimately rejected here as well, Jesus reproached this prosperous crossroad city. Save for its synagogue ruins, the remnants of the house of Peter, little else remains.—*Mk 1:21; Lk 4:31-32.*

The Pool of Siloam — Hezekieh ordered a tunnel cut underground during the Assyrian siege of Jerusalem, in an attempt to bring much-needed water within the city walls (2 Chronicles 32:30). Two teams armed with picks went burrowing down, hoping to meet, relying on voice contact—and did. This engineering victory saved the city and resulted in this reservoir spring of Siloam. It is believed that Jesus healed the man born blind here—*Jn 9:1-11.*

The Sacred Stairway — The Assumptionist Fathers of St. Peter in Gallicantu (Cock-crow) Church excavated an ancient flight of steps at this site, believed to be the house and prison of the high priest Caiaphas. Within the city walls in the time of Jesus, these steps are the shortest way from Gethsemane to the upper city of Jerusalem—*Lk 22:54-71.*

The Via Dolorosa — The Via Dolorosa composes the fourteen Stations of the Cross. Nine of these Stations are found in the Gospel, and five in tradition. The Stations are found within churches and chapels, as well as along the city streets, from the Lithostrotos to Golgotha. Processions led by the Franciscan Fathers still occur every Friday afternoon, at 3:00 P.M.

The Mount of Olives — The Mount of Olives offers a superb panorama of the mountains of Moab, the Dead Sea, the Judean Hills, and the Old City of Jerusalem. On this Mount are the most extensive of Jewish cemeteries, the sacred shrines of the Garden and Church of Gethsemane, the Russian Church of St. Mary Magdalene, and the Dominus Flevit (The Lord Wept) Chapel and the chapel of the Ascension. Each Palm Sunday finds hundreds of the local faithful winding down this valley with palms, and entering the city gates with prayers and hymns.

MAGNIFICENT EDITIONS THAT BELONG IN EVERY CATHOLIC HOME

WHEREVER CATHOLIC BOOKS ARE SOLD